Advance Praise for

Teen Dating Violence

"As the mother of four teenage daughters, ages 11, 14, 16, and 17, I think this book is required reading for both parents and teens."

Donna Gasior, Burbank, IL

"*Teen Dating Violence* provides valuable resources for those working with young people. Through the use of personal stories and current research data, the author raises our consciousness regarding the causes and consequences of dating violence. The book captures the effects dating violence has on those involved and on our society."

Teresa LeCompte, teacher, Mother McAuley Liberal Arts High School, Chicago

"Dr. Sanders' work on date rape and date violence makes visible another, frequently hidden, form of violence. Dating violence affects the lives of an estimated one-third to two-thirds of our children, adolescents, and young adults. Yet, little research has been conducted on this subject, limiting knowledge and understanding of the nature and scope of the issues and care needed by the victims and their families. Through the use of stories of real life situations, Dr. Sanders gives voice to these victims and their family members. She also highlights the need for competent, compassionate care and for social and legal policy reform."

Mary Lebold, Dean of School of Nursing, Saint Xavier University, Chicago

"Clear and insightful, this is a solidly researched book with startling implications for teens and those involved with guiding them through this often treacherous life passage. As a seasoned clinician, I had a wake up call after reading this book! If you think there are no differences between violence against women and teenage girls, and the way in which these differences are handled in our social, educational, and criminal justice systems, you need to read this book!"

Judith Kelly, Licensed Clinical Social Worker, Oak Lawn, IL

Teen Dating
Violence

AC SS — Adolescent Cultures, School & Society

Joseph L. DeVitis & Linda Irwin-DeVitis
General Editors

Vol. 24

PETER LANG
New York • Washington, D.C./Baltimore • Bern
Frankfurt am Main • Berlin • Brussels • Vienna • Oxford

Susan M. Sanders

Teen Dating
Violence

The Invisible Peril

PETER LANG
New York • Washington, D.C./Baltimore • Bern
Frankfurt am Main • Berlin • Brussels • Vienna • Oxford

Library of Congress Cataloging-in-Publication Data

Sanders, Susan M. (Susan Mary).
Teen dating violence: the invisible peril / Susan M. Sanders.
p. cm. — (Adolescent cultures, school and society; vol. 24)
Includes bibliographical references and index.
1. Dating violence. 2. Dating violence—United States. 3. Teenage girls—
Abuse of—United States. 4. Abusive men—United States. I. Title.
II. Adolescent cultures, school & society; vol. 24.
HQ801.83 .S36   362.88—dc21   2001038910
ISBN 0-8204-5762-0
ISSN 1091-1464

Die Deutsche Bibliothek-CIP-Einheitsaufnahme

Sanders, Susan M.:
Teen dating violence: the invisible peril / Susan M. Sanders.
−New York; Washington, D.C./Baltimore; Bern;
Frankfurt am Main; Berlin; Brussels; Vienna; Oxford: Lang.
(Adolescent cultures, school and society; Vol. 24)
ISBN 0-8204-5762-0

Cover design by Dutton & Sherman Design

The paper in this book meets the guidelines for permanence and durability
of the Committee on Production Guidelines for Book Longevity
of the Council of Library Resources.

To

Mom, Dad, and Unc

They were always there

for each of us

CONTENTS

ACKNOWLEDGMENTS

Trained in policy analysis and public policy, I always thought I would write a book on nonprofit organizations and the role that trust plays in helping them function effectively. I never thought I would write a book on teen dating violence.

I did not know much about the problem of domestic violence among adult partners, much less among teens, until my religious community, the Sisters of Mercy of the Regional Community of Chicago, undertook an initiative to respond to domestic violence. From these women, I learned about the violence that was being inflicted on many of the people whom we serve in our ministries. I also learned that many of the women who serve with us in our hospitals and educational institutions sometimes come to work after being beaten or abused.

Now I know a little more about the problems of these women. However, I certainly knew nothing about the violence that was being inflicted on young teenage women—both elementary and high school students—some of whom I taught in our own high schools. Not until I met Kathy Clarke, one of my former students, who had become a noted domestic violence counselor and advocate for victims of domestic violence, did I learn about the violence that sometimes erupts in teen dating relationships.

Kathy shared a draft of her book *The Breakable Vow*. It was a powerful story. Subsequently, we introduced the book into twelve Chicago area high schools when we collaborated on the Dating Violence Curriculum Intervention Project (DVCIP), a project that we piloted in those schools. It was from this collaboration that Kathy was able to introduce her book and the curriculum to a broader audience of high school students and teachers, and I was able to collect the survey data that became the source material for much of this book. My thanks to Kathy for making important contributions to teens involved in violent dating relationships and for helping me to commit to writing this book.

However, moving from ideas to programs and research takes funding. Without grants from the Sisters of Mercy, the Agatha O'Brien Ministry Fund, and DePaul University, the time and resources to conduct the survey and interview research would not have been available. I thank each of these groups for demonstrating a commitment to improving the lives of women and children that goes far beyond pious exhortation.

In the process of writing this book, I have met some wonderful people and relied on the skills and generosity of many friends and family members. One of these is Tom Santoro, a man whose dedication to the cause of preventing teen dating violence engages him in the daily process of remembering and recounting the tragic story of his daughter's death. He is a model of energy, compassion, and commitment. I am grateful to him for giving his permission to use his story in this book, and to Teresa LeCompte, who not only told me about Tom's work but also, through her own writing, showed me that it was possible to complete this book.

Then there are the women who shared their stories with me. Known only to the readers as Maggie, Alissa, and Alejandra, because using their real names could put them in danger of retribution from their former boyfriends, these women put flesh on what can often be the dull reporting of statistical information. I am grateful to them for giving me permission to use their stories, even though I cannot acknowledge them by name. I hope that the prospect of helping young women like themselves is a sufficient recognition of their contributions.

The Minnesota Program Development, Inc., was also generous in giving permission to use its material. Specifically, through the Domestic Abuse Intervention Project, the Minnesota Program gave permission to use the text from the "Power and Control Equality Wheels" that were developed by battered women in Duluth. Materials for this project include a poster-size representation of these wheels, which are part of an educational curriculum *Power and Control: Tactics of Men Who Batter.* These materials are available from Minnesota Program Development, Inc., 202 East Superior Street, Duluth, MN 55802.

A similar kindness was extended to me by the Project for Victims of Family Violence, Inc., in Fayetteville, Arkansas. *Signs to Look for in a Battering Personality* is a most helpful, quick reference list to discuss with teenage women and men. I am grateful for the permission to use it in this book.

Among the friends who helped me produce this work are those who researched, reviewed, critiqued, or edited it. Thank you to Mary Sheehan, RSM, PhD, who, as a professional psychologist, closely read the text for lapses of logic and unsubstantiated conclusions, and helped me avoid pop psychologizing about causal relationships. Additional thanks go to Mary Apcel, Melissa Apcel, Patrick J. Butler, Joy Clough, RSM, Sheila King, Susan Kosinski, Kathy Mareska, Betsy Meisenheimer, Kathleen Moriarty, RSM, Mark Rasar, Noelle Butler Reed, and Carole Wilson who, as editors, typists, indexers, formatters, proofreaders, or promoters, nudged me toward clearer and shorter sentences and a tighter organizational structure. Then there is Heidi Burns, my editor at Peter Lang Publishing, Inc. How fortunate—and surprised—I was to hear her enthusiasm for the topic, especially at a time when I was questioning the relevance of most of what I was writing. She was a bright spot in a long winter of writing and revising.

I am grateful to those who worked as research assistants and "gofers," especially Jane Lee, Barbara O'Toole, Nancy Pepper, Yvette Perez, and Cathy Yanikoski. Elaine Schuster, PhD, and Corinne Raven, RSM, kindly helped introduce me to some of the high school principals who agreed to participate in the study. Furthermore, for their cooperation, enthusiasm, and interest in helping young women, I want to thank the principals, teachers, and counselors at the twelve pilot schools for being willing to let yet one more academic disrupt the routine in their classrooms to conduct research.

Finally, I want to remember my parents and my uncle for their interest in my research. Although my mom, Mary or "Sis" Sanders was the first to read, with genuine interest, earlier drafts of this book, she never saw it in its completed form. Nor did my uncle, Msgr. Martin J. O'Day, who kept me focused on the task through his daily prayers and queries, "Is it done yet?" Before both he and my mom died, I was able to report to them that, "Yes, it is finished. At least the text is written." And they, as usual, were happy to celebrate this accomplishment with me. The same would have been true for my dad, Ray Sanders, who preceded them in death three years earlier. When he heard my early findings, such evidence of abuse sickened and infuriated him. How could any parents ignore their child's—any child's—plea for help? It was incomprehensible to him. I know that my mom, dad, and uncle would welcome any efforts to protect children and teens from those who would abuse them or rob them of their innocence, their wonder, or their enthusiasm for life.

My mom, dad, and uncle were always there for both my brother John and me, as they were for many other kids who played Little League, hung out in our family kitchen, or sat on the front steps of the house on summer evenings. Simply put, they were committed to "being there" for us, usually hanging around and, later, even hanging out with us. They made comments, asked questions and, sometimes, we even answered them. As adults, they did not always get it right, at least by our juvenile standards, but there is no doubt they did right by us. Thanks, Mom, Dad, and Unc.

As I watch my three nieces Kate, Colleen, and Maureen grow in beauty and grace, I take pride in knowing that they too are lucky enough to know the watchful eye of good parents like John and Mary who are committed to "being there" for each of them. Would that all young women and young men could be as fortunate in experiencing the power of a loving and active adult presence.

INTRODUCTION

THE INVISIBLE PERIL

"Why study that? It's kids' stuff. The things you are labeling violent and abusive are just part of the process of kids' learning to work through relationships with the opposite sex."

"Aren't you making a mountain out of a molehill? Aren't the girls just being overly sensitive? Aren't you trying to solve a problem that really doesn't exist? If it does, is it really that big of a deal?"

A friend of mine, the father of four girls, had asked me about this research. When I told him I was studying teenage dating violence, particularly the violence that males inflict on young teenage women, he was unusually critical. "How bad can it be anyway?" he wanted to know.

Indeed, he had raised some important questions. What is teen dating violence? How does it compare in its causes, in its characteristics, and in its effects to intimate partner violence between adults? How pervasive is it? How have the law enforcement, civic, and educational communities responded to it? How effective have these responses been? What can we learn from teens themselves about how to make better policy responses to the abuse or violence that many young teenage women will encounter while dating?

Teen violence, like domestic violence, occurs when a dating or intimate partner's action causes emotional distress for the victim, when the perpetrator threatens or causes physical harm to the partner, or when the aggressor forces his partner to engage in sexual acts against her will.[1] In its causes, characteristics, and effects, teen dating violence mirrors domestic violence between adults. The causes of teen dating violence, for example, like the causes of domestic violence, are typically found in the perpetrator's desire for power and control. Further, the characteristics of teen dating violence mimic the same patterns and cycles of abuse that profile domestic violence between adults.

The effects of teen dating violence on the abused, whether of an emotionally, physically, or sexually abusive nature, are felt immediately and are often borne far into the future. These effects may include the erosion of the victim's self-esteem as well as difficulties in developing meaningful and healthy relationships later in life.

How pervasive is teen dating violence? This question is difficult to answer, but one estimate suggests that almost 19 percent of teenage high school women experienced some form of physical or sexual abuse while dating.[2] Moreover, because it excludes emotional violence, because teens are reluctant to reveal their involvement in a violent dating relationship, and because of the methodological difficulties of conducting research directly with teens, it is likely that these figures, as well as those from other research efforts, are underestimated. While the scope of the incidence may be in dispute, what cannot be disputed is that intimate partner abuse among teens is pervasive, is brutal, and sometimes is lethal.

How have the law enforcement, civic, and educational communities responded to teen dating violence? The answer is twofold. First, apart from date rape, there are many public officials who do not know or believe that dating relationships among teens are sometimes physically and emotionally violent. As researchers conduct more studies of teen dating violence, and as law enforcement communities begin to gather information on intimate partner violence that differentiates violence involving teens from that involving adults, the data will make it more difficult to ignore the problem, or to dismiss the behaviors as "puppy love," or as the typical difficulties teenagers experience in dating. Moreover, it will be harder to point fingers at young women who, some would argue, "asked for it." Second, among those who believe that a problem exists among teens, many public policies and programmatic approaches to the problem of teen dating violence are ineffective because they do not take into account the unique circumstances of minors who try to access the legal system or social services. Thus, if a "one-size-fits-all" policy and programmatic approach to domestic violence addresses teens as well as adults, then minors lack meaningful redress and access. Further, such an approach promotes a false sense of security among policy makers who believe that the problem of teen dating violence is being addressed when, in actuality, it is not. In either case, whether because of a lack of information or a false perception, the invisible peril remains invisible, perilous, and unaddressed.

What can we learn from young teenage women themselves about how to make better policy or programmatic responses to the violence that many of them encounter while dating? Rather than collecting data from adults who have been asked to recall their dating experiences as teens, collecting data from teenage women themselves is a more salient strategy for designing policies and programs appropriate to them. Without data gathered directly from young teenage women themselves, policy makers and social service program directors will continue to craft policies that, while well intentioned, do not quite fit the situation of a young woman who cannot leave home or school to escape an abusive boyfriend.

What is normal when it relates to teen dating? It is difficult, if not impossible, to define something whose meaning is as unique as each couple engaged in a dating relationship. While we may not be able to define easily what is normal, we know one thing for sure: Teen dating violence is not normal, nor is it about love. It is not the consequence of mistakes typically made by those new to dating or the result of lewd behavior on the part of young women. Rather, as my research and the research of others show, teen dating violence is a pattern of systematic emotional, physical, or sexual control and abuse that a boyfriend forces upon his dating partner. Unfortunately, as the research in this book will illustrate, a sizable number of young women do not recognize their involvement in a violent dating relationship. Moreover, they frequently mistake abusive behavior for love.

This book will show that teen dating violence is a social problem, one very different from domestic violence. As such, I argue that it deserves a different policy response, one that recognizes that most young teenage women who are involved in teen dating violence are not adults but minors. Because they are minors, they do not have the same rights and means of redress as adult women.

In view of the differences between teen dating violence and domestic violence, what might adults and policy makers do to respond more appropriately to teens involved in violent dating relationships? As a first step, adults who work directly with teens, whether as parents, teachers, or counselors, should learn to recognize the signs of teen dating violence. The first two chapters of this book illustrate the symptoms of teen dating violence as viewed from the perspectives of those who have been abused and from those who counsel and assist them in their recoveries. These two chapters provide information that teens and parents can use to evaluate the appropriateness of what teens may be experiencing while dating. Because Chapter One includes the "in their own words" stories of three people who experienced teen dating violence and its effects, the text can be used as case studies to help teens learn the symptoms and cycles of teen dating violence.

As a second step to making better responses to teen dating violence, those whose work indirectly affects the lives of teens, especially those working in policy areas, should understand the subtle but important differences between teen dating violence and domestic violence. Chapter Three outlines these differences from developmental, legal, and programmatic perspectives. With a better knowledge of the current limitations of public policy, policy makers will be better able to craft policies and programs more appropriate to the age and circumstances of young teenage women and those who abuse them.

A third step toward making better responses to teenage women involved in emotionally, physically, or sexually abusive relationships concerns the methods that researchers and policy analysts currently use to collect data about teen dating violence. Probably more for teen dating violence than for many other areas of research, the conclusion that "more research is needed" is an understatement. Whereas Chapter Four reviews some of the research on teen dating violence, the conclusions drawn from these studies are frequently hampered by methodological and ethical obstacles researchers encounter when conducting research with minors. The result is that researchers frequently substitute retrospective research with adults, who are asked to recall their experiences as teens, for interviews and surveys with the minors. From this analysis, Chapter Four takes a normative turn. It is here, and again in the conclusion, that I exhort policy researchers to take the time to collect data from those who most directly suffer from the social problem being addressed. In the case of teen dating violence, it is the opinions and experiences of the young women and young men themselves that should be solicited.

We can "talk the talk," and we know that talk is cheap. So Chapters Five and Six attempt to "walk the walk" by featuring the opinions and experiences of 499 female high school juniors. Although these young women came from a variety of socioeconomic, cultural, and racial backgrounds, all were under the age of 18 at the time they were surveyed, and each subsequently participated in a teen dating violence curriculum intervention project (DVCIP) at their high schools. Similarly to domestic violence, the survey data indicate that teen dating violence does not discriminate by race, culture, or socioeconomic background. Further, the data denote substantial confusion among the young women about how to evaluate and respond to the ostensibly disrespectful or violent behaviors they experience at the hands of their boyfriends. Should young women break up with boyfriends who force them to have sex? Is stalking a sign of love and commitment? If young women want to break up, how often do they hear their boyfriends threaten to harm themselves, their girlfriends, or others? For a significant number of young women in the sample, these are just a few of the questions without clear answers. If teens do experience violence at the hands of their boyfriends, will they turn to others for help? If so, to whom and under what circumstances?

Perhaps to the surprise of many adults, the data presented in Chapter Seven suggest that teens will talk to others, both adults and peers, about their dating problems, especially when physical violence begins to manifest itself. Unfortunately, teens also have a number of reasons to fear talking to adults. Their comments suggest that even well-intentioned adults can unconsciously set up a number of barriers to fruitful dialogue between teens and themselves. The responses of the young women to my survey provide some insights into what adults, especially parents, teachers, and counselors, can do to make teens more trusting and less fearful about talking about their involvement in an abusive relationship.

The book concludes with Chapter Eight, a discussion of policy and programmatic responses to teen dating violence. Based upon survey data and interviews with those who have been abused or with those who have worked with them, I argue that the ambivalence that young teenage women have about whether they are being abused suggests the need for education about what constitutes emotional, physical, or sexual abuse. Without some sense of what is happening to them, how can young teenage women take the steps necessary to protect themselves from those who would use or abuse them?

In addition to the survey data that I collected from the young women themselves, I interviewed adults who experienced violence during their teen dating relationships. Furthermore, I also talked with parents, teachers, school administrators, and domestic violence counselors. Their stories and their observations provide a context and a level of detail that substantiate the findings from the survey data.

While important, there are two aspects of teen dating violence that I do not cover in this book. The first is the teen dating violence experienced among homosexual partners. The second is the violence that males experience at the hands of their female partners.

In both instances, my research was constrained more by a lack of resources to study these problems than by lack of interest or a belief that such expressions of intimate partner violence are nonexistent or unimportant. Given these resource constraints, I made the decision to limit the scope of this research to the dating violence young women who are minors experience at the hands of their boyfriends. In making such a decision, I also add credence to the reality that the frequency and severity of the violence that young women experience while dating males is much greater than in other types of intimate partner relationships.

Teen dating violence is not as visible to the community as is the massive and graphic violence that occurred in the school shootings at Paducah, Columbine, Santee, or El Cajon. It does not command the same degree of attention as do drive-by shootings or gang killings; it is not limited to date rape; and it is not always accompanied by excessive drinking or drugs. Rather, teen dating violence is often a private, invisible peril. Typically, it occurs between two individuals and does not take place in a school or social setting. Moreover, it can escalate from behaviors that one may construe only as disrespectful to behaviors that are physically abusive or even life-threatening.

Is teen dating violence an epidemic? As the data in this book will reveal, the answer to this question is as much a matter of definition and data as it is debate. Compared to the spread of the AIDS virus in southern Africa, it would be hard to call teen dating violence an epidemic. However, compared to other social problems such as gang violence, drug addiction, alcohol abuse, and teenage suicide, the incidence of teen dating violence suggests that it is also a pervasive social problem and, depending on how it is defined and measured, afflicts *at least* three percent, but probably many more, of the young women under the age of eighteen.

If teen dating violence is a problem affecting a significant proportion of young women in the United States, then why is it so invisible to so many parents, teachers, and other adults concerned with the welfare of young men and women? Unfortunately, what holds true for many adults also resonates for many young teenage women: Problems remain invisible when they are not recognized as problems.

Sadly, the data from my research suggest that many young teenage women do not themselves recognize the problem of dating violence in their own relationships. Specifically, teen dating violence exists and remains invisible because many young women do not have a clue about how to evaluate the normalcy or appropriateness of their boyfriends' dating behaviors. With conflicting frames of reference against which to assess roles and behaviors between dating partners, and without normative guidance from adults, they cannot differentiate disrespect, mistrust, and emotional, physical, or sexual abuse from respectful, trusting, affectionate, and loving behaviors, behaviors that enhance and celebrate the dignity of each dating partner. Given a lack of worldly experience and awareness of what is normal or appropriate in a teen dating relationship, the physical and emotional health of many young women is imperiled by teen dating violence, an invisible peril that tracks its victims as surely as any teenage shooter or gangland warlord.

CHAPTER 1

THE FACES OF TEEN
DATING VIOLENCE

"Even now, nearly three years later, I still cannot forget how frightened I was. . . ."

How do young teenage girls become involved in violent dating relationships? What do they see in their dates, and what do they think about themselves such that a dating relationship can become frightening to recall, even three years later? When violence strikes, how do family members recall the loss and reclaim their lives after an ex-boyfriend murders their teenage daughter? How can dating violence that begins in one's teenage years become domestic violence in a marital setting? How are the scars of domestic violence transmitted from one generation of abusers to the next?

Before the book profiles teen dating violence in a general sense, this chapter shares the stories of three people who were either involved in violent dating relationships while they were teens, or who suffered the tragedy of burying a daughter who was a victim of teen dating violence. Although each of these stories is unique to the individuals involved, taken together they describe elements and patterns common to teen dating violence.

Maggie's Story: A Study in Confusion, Self-doubt, and Abuse

"Maggie's Story,"[1] illustrates how confused a young woman can become when she encounters an abusive dating partner. Maggie details not only her confusion but also the lessons she learned about herself that have helped her build subsequent healthy dating relationships and prevented her from again becoming involved with abusive boyfriends.

I met Mark when I was waitressing. I was accustomed to keeping my eye out for cute guys my age. I wanted a boyfriend and was tired of bouncing from person to person and the failure that accompanied it. Mark and I began to hang out on a regular basis, usually at my apartment, which was a trash heap but had an open door for partying and good times any hour of the night.

My roommate had her love interest. I developed mine with Mark. The four of us would meet religiously to laugh, to watch movies, to listen to music, and to get high. Things took off too fast from that point on. Eventually, I grew tired of the nightly routine, and I began to notice something in Mark that I did not like.

Prior to our relationship, Mark had been a Harley motorcycle rider who had taken a nasty fall. He gave up riding permanently for fear of crashing again. I replaced his love for motorcycles. I was in charge of making him feel needed, loved, and secure. Yet, with a full-time job, school, homework, and friends to associate with, I just could not—I did not want—to give him the attention he needed.

We talked and agreed that it would be good for both of us to have our own interests. It was at that point that I began to become insecure, and Mark began to ride his bike again.

He started hanging around with his old riding friends, and new adventures with him opened up to feed my dangerous side. We went four-wheeling and car racing. I began to feel that our relationship was exactly what I had always wanted. Then, one day, one event shattered my image of Mark—and us—irreparably.

Mark's best friend Bob was looking for Mark one afternoon. Bob came to my apartment to wait for Mark. As Bob was waiting in my living room for Mark to call, he began to tell me how often Mark would lie and how good he was at it. Mark's grandmother had told me the same thing about her grandson. She had warned me about him and said he was a 'pathological liar.'

I told Bob that I did not believe either him or Mark's grandmother, and that he should give me an example. So Bob gave me one.

He asked me if Mark had told me recently that he had to leave my house in a hurry because his—that is Bob's—father had died and that Mark wanted to be with him. That was true, I told him. Well, Bob told me that his father was not dead. Rather, Mark had just made up the story so he could leave with an excuse to go over to Bob's house to help him rebuild his Corvette. The look on his face told me that even the cruelest of people would not joke around about a father's death in that way. I told Bob to leave, and not long afterwards, Mark called.

By the time Mark arrived at my apartment, I had all of his things packed up in bags. When he rang the doorbell, I brought all of his stuff down with me and put it in his car. I knew that he had never suspected that I could ever break up with him. When I did, he punched the steering wheel and his car window so hard that he broke two of his knuckles. He then ran out of the car across a very busy main street—without looking—and disappeared for half an hour. I went inside and told my roommate what had happened. And then I knew that I could not end it with him because he seemed to care so much. When he returned, we talked; we made up.

The next morning, I told Mark that I could never feel as secure with him again. That seemed to set him off. In my room, there was a windowshade that anyone who had ever been to my apartment had signed. Mark said he wanted to write something on it (he had refused for the first few months). He made me leave the room. When I walked back into the room, expecting to see something very romantic on the shade, I read a short sentence. It said that I would not have to worry about anything anymore because he would not be around after that day.

I ripped down the shade, and Mark started crying. I told him, in a fit of fury, that he could do whatever he wanted to after he was done with driving me to the store and replacing my shade. Then, without warning, Mark ran out of my apartment. I didn't have any shoes on, and didn't have time to grab my keys. I begged Mark to slow down. He would not, so I grabbed on to the tail of his shirt as he ran down the stairs and out the door. I did not let go of him. I felt myself falling. He pushed me off of him and I fell hard onto the concrete. I scraped much of the skin off one arm and one leg. I began to hyperventilate, and Mark carried me back upstairs. All this occurred in front of two apartment buildings and my neighbors.

Things went downhill fast after that. Mark's car broke down. He asked me to loan him $300 to buy a new one. Since I was still waitressing, I had cash on hand. Mark knew this: Every night that I worked, he would come in an hour before we closed and watch me count tip money to see how well I did. When he ran out of money, I was the first person he would seek for 'advice.' Technically, he never asked me to support him financially, but his stories about his predicaments could almost force a caring individual into giving him extra cash to help.

By the end of our 10-month relationship, I had loaned him $1000 for what seemed to be unavoidable circumstances. Mark needed money for a car. Mark needed money for insurance and car repairs. Mark needed money for marijuana. Mark needed money to pay bills, to buy necessities, to pay tickets, to pay off debts.

Each time, I wrote him a check, and each time, I made it clear that it was a loan. But I have never received one penny of the money he owes me. It has been almost three years.

In between fights, Mark and I still enjoyed each other's company, which is why I stayed with him. During breakups, Mark used hard drugs, threatened to move out of state, and claimed that he would commit suicide. I went back every time. We broke up four or five times. According to Mark, each time was due to my insecurity or my pestering. On one occasion, Mark had his best friend call me at work to end our relationship. Mark was never able to say to my face that he did not want to be with me. I took this to be that he truly cared about me in a way that he was unable to express.

Toward the end of our relationship, Mark would typically cancel plans by leaving me notes on my car. Or he would leave messages on my answering machine when he knew I was not home. I cannot count the number of times he would tell me to be somewhere at a certain time, and then not be there. He would 'forget.' Or he would tell me to come over after work, but then, when I showed up, he would close his windows, turn his air conditioner on full blast, turn his television set up, and turn off his lights so I could not see him. A number of times, I would return home without seeing him because he 'fell asleep' and did not hear me or the phone.

During one 'conversation' with him, he yelled at me, called me a bitch while on the telephone with his friend and, after hanging up the phone, grabbed his bike and told me to wait there for him. I asked him why he was taking his bike. He said not to worry about it. I stood in front of the door and said I would not let him leave until he explained why he was taking the bike. Then he got crazy. He told me I was lucky that I was his girlfriend or he would have thrown me over the balcony. He then told me that if I did not move, he would 'plow right over me' with his bike. I scoffed at him and told him that I was not afraid.

As soon as I got home, almost five hours later, I had a message from him apologizing and asking me to drive back over to his house. I did. Often, after fights, it would go like this. He would apologize and, to avoid additional confrontation, he would send me a rose or write me a poem or a little note saying how much he loved me.

It was because I was so confused and lost that I stayed with him through all of this. I did not know that I was worth much more than I was receiving. So, I allowed someone who claimed to love me to treat me like garbage. He threatened me when I broke up with him, and he was a threat to me as a boyfriend. I just could not get away from him.

Part of the problem was me. I had my own insecurities, ingrained from prior relationships. I was jealous of his friends and feared that they were more important to him than I was. I gave him money and sex every time he wanted or needed me so that I could have a bond with him, if only a weak one. I allowed Mark to exploit my caring nature and doubted my good instincts about when he was lying. He used my naivete to his advantage and claimed that nothing was wrong, that all my concerns were figments of my imagination, and that they were too ridiculous even to talk about. He threatened me when I broke up with him.

The final straw came as a blow to both him and me. I was short of cash one month and needed some money back from Mark to pay my bills. He had entirely wiped out my savings account, and my checking ledger included his name on several checks as well.

Mark told me to wait so he could call his estranged father, who had cosigned on his bank certificates so that he could not touch them without permission. It was because of these CDs that I always felt secure in loaning him money. I knew he had money, so I thought he would repay me. A few weeks earlier, Mark had told me he had visited his father and patched things up with him, so I was hopeful. However, the next day Mark told me his father would not cosign for him.

A few days later, we broke up and I did not hear from him. I drove all his things over to his grandmother's apartment, and left them there with a note for him. I still did not hear anything. Finally, on Father's Day, no less, I contacted Mark's father. I explained my situation and pleaded with him to cosign to help both Mark and me. Mark's father told me he didn't know what I was talking about and that he had not spoken to Mark in years. He said he had never cosigned for Mark on CDs, and that he would not help me.

Some days later, I told Mark about my conversation with his father. I told him that I now knew he had been lying to me. His response? He called me names at the top of his voice. He said I was a waste of time. However, not long after that, we were back together again. Mark had made a phone call to another friend to get a loan to pay me back. The evening he was supposed to drop off my money at the apartment, he never came. I waited for one hour and then drove to his apartment. I was 20 minutes into the drive before I pulled over and asked myself what I was doing. It was then that I knew I had had enough.

I turned around and went home, and have never attempted to contact Mark since. He still has my money. But I had lost more than money. I had lost a substantial amount of weight, down from my 100 pounds. I barely slept due to late night car rides and fights. I was never really happy, and I was constantly wondering what he would do next. I became completely detached from reality. Mark had twisted my mind so badly that I couldn't even remember what happened and what had not. I was smoking, losing energy for school and work. I began to hate my life and no longer wanted to live. My friends were wise and supportive, but I could not make sense of their advice. I was left without Mark, with no money, no sense of worth, no sense of reality, and no closure. This all started when I was in my teens. Now I am 20 years old.

The relationship between Maggie and Mark started innocently enough, sharing time and activities together. They met to watch movies, to listen to music and, sometimes, to get high. Soon, however, these pastimes became dull, and Maggie and Mark replaced them with more daring adventures with cars and motorcycles. However, even these pastimes, though signaling self-destructive behavior, were not sentinel events for teen dating violence. Lying to one's partner, however, is. Mark's grandmother had warned Maggie about it, and Bob had confirmed it. Moreover, punching steering wheels so hard as to break knuckles, writing threats of suicide on windowshades, driving recklessly to scare others, borrowing money without repayment, consistently standing up a date, and threatening physical harm to one's partner are also abusive behaviors in a dating relationship.

Why did Maggie keep returning to such an apparently unseemly and abusive dating partner? In reflecting on her relationship to Mark and on her relationships with Mark's two predecessors, Maggie clearly recognized her own responsibility in these dysfunctional and abusive relationships. She wanted to prove that she could "get the guy" that everyone else wanted. She enjoyed engaging in being a rebellious teenager, although some forms of her rebellion, such as drug use and driving in speeding cars, were more self-destructive than rebellious. Mark's lying, while a major irritation, did not seem to be sufficiently serious to Maggie until it became a pattern.

However, Maggie should have suspected that something was very wrong with her relationship to Mark when physically intimidating and violent behavior became the norm. No, Maggie, it is not normal for a man to break his knuckles by slamming them on the steering wheel. No, Maggie, it is not normal to threaten suicide or physical harm to another. No, Maggie, a young woman does not deserve to be manipulated for money or even be kept waiting by a date.

Yes, Maggie, you were insecure, and you could not let go. You thought Mark would change. Worse yet, you thought that you could change him. All of these ideas were misguided, but none of them indicated that you "deserved" the manipulative and abusive behavior you experienced while dating during your teens.

After Maggie and Mark parted company, Maggie was better able to reflect objectively on the ups and downs of their "roller-coaster" relationship. After the fact, it was clearer to her that there were clues and triggers indicating that their relationship was an abusive one. Having "been there" was not a good place to be, but Maggie's dating experience with Mark has enabled her to seek more positive self-affirming relationships.

Mark surprised Maggie by his sudden violent outburst in the car. Maggie then had to answer a difficult question: Was this sudden outburst one incident of aberrant behavior, or was it the beginning of a pattern?

For most young women, the question is easier to answer if the violent outburst occurs on a first date rather than later in the relationship. In an informal poll, 75 percent of the high school women questioned said they would never date a guy again who exhibited violent behavior on the first date. However, when asked if they would break up with a partner if the first violent outburst had occurred after three months of dating, the percentage was reversed: 75 percent of the young women said they would *not* break up and 25 percent said they would.[2] Indeed, it is difficult to know whether initial outbursts are aberrations or the beginning of a pattern of abuse.

Despite the longevity of their relationship, Maggie had exercised good instincts in separating from Mark. Lisa Santoro also separated from her boyfriend. Though the circumstances were quite different—Lisa had experienced some controlling behavior but not physical or sexual violence—she, like Maggie, also broke up with her boyfriend. In contrast to Mark, however, Lisa's boyfriend began to stalk her and to plot her murder after they had broken up.

One month after her high school graduation, Lisa was beaten to death by her ex-boyfriend, who bludgeoned her with a baseball bat. Lisa's father Tom tells her story—and his—and how he has translated his sorrow into a very successful teen dating violence prevention program called "Dear Lisa."[3]

"Dear Lisa": Murder by an Ex-boyfriend

I was sitting in the bleachers on the 50-yard line of our high school football field. It was a warm sunny day, and the second quarter was nearly over. We were ahead. I didn't really notice until later, but no one was sitting near me. Then the half came to a close and people started walking around, getting food and drinks. And the cheerleaders came onto the field and started doing their cheers. When the cheerleaders had finished, the poms took the field. It was then that I heard over the public address that their routine would be dedicated to the memory of Lisa Santoro.

Lisa was my daughter. And though her parting prayer for her classmates on the day of their high school commencement was for 'ending violence in our world,' she herself would die a little over one month later, murdered by an ex-boyfriend who had beaten her to death with a baseball bat.

As I watched the poms go through their routine, I was crying and hoping that someone would come up to me and put their arm around me. No one did.

In January, 1994, Lisa started to date a guy who lived a few miles away. His name was "Dan." He was a year older and didn't attend the same high school as Lisa. In the five months Lisa dated this guy, I never really understood why she was attracted to him. He was quiet and average looking. I would say that they were almost opposites of each other. After Lisa's death, someone asked me if I liked him. I didn't like him. I didn't dislike him. To me, he had no personality. He was just there.

Around June, when Lisa started to work at the swimming pool, she met another guy who was in charge of the pool. His name was "Paul." He was better looking, but more importantly, he was Lisa's type, always laughing, joking, wanting to enjoy life and have fun. It was around graduation time, and I knew that Lisa was going to be breaking up with Dan. I'm sure Paul had a lot to do with it. Shortly after, Lisa did break up with Dan.

Dan tried to get Lisa to go back to him, but Lisa had her mind made up. She started to date Paul. One time, Paul was going downtown to get sworn in for his citizenship, and Lisa was going to go with him. Dan found out and asked Lisa if she would go with him for some surgery that he needed. So Lisa went with Dan. It turned out that there was no surgery. It was just Dan's way of getting Lisa away from Paul. Later, we also found out that it was then that Dan started to plan Lisa's death.

On July 27th, Dan called Lisa and asked her to go out to exchange letters they had written to each other when they were dating. Lisa agreed to meet Dan on the 28th. At that time, I didn't know they were going to be together. I was on duty that day at the firehouse and was scheduled to work a 24-hour shift. My wife informed me that Lisa was going out with Dan that night and that she couldn't wait until he was out of Lisa's life for good. I came home about 6 p.m. and gave Lisa a kiss and went back to the firehouse.

About 1 a.m. that evening, I got a call from my wife. Lisa wasn't home and she was supposed to be home at midnight. I came home from the firehouse, tried calling the house where Lisa was supposed to be, and got a satanic recording. I told my wife that I was going to take a ride to the house to look for Lisa. When I got to the house, I saw the police car and the ambulance in front. I knew my Lisa was dead.

I left the scene and went to the police station. I didn't know what I was supposed to do. I drove home to tell my wife and son that Lisa was not coming home. The ex-boyfriend had murdered our Lisa.

Many phone calls and tears later, the next day dawned and it was time to make arrangements for the funeral. Plus we had to find a cemetery. In the afternoon, we got a phone call from the coroner's office to come in to identify our Lisa. That was one trip we were not looking forward to.

The day of the wake, we were still walking around in a daze, not believing this had happened. Arriving at the funeral home and entering the room where Lisa was at rest cannot be described—seeing our Lisa lying in a coffin, looking like an angel. . . .

The next morning, we got ready for the funeral. Picking out a tie to match a suit didn't really matter too much to me. I just wanted to see my angel again. When we arrived at the funeral home, people were already there, and we sat and watched as more friends came to pay their last respects to Lisa. There were hundreds. The funeral procession was a mile long. At the grave site, many of Lisa's friends did not want to leave.

After the services, my wife Barb and I took off work for a couple of weeks. We mailed out hundreds of thank you cards and, of course, visited Lisa every day. We also had to start getting ourselves ready to go to court. The ex-boyfriend was charged with first-degree murder.

Going to court once a month drained both of us. It took a lot of energy just to get up each day, let alone going to court to see the ex-boyfriend sitting only 30 feet away.

They told us ahead of time that he was going to plead not guilty. It happens in about 75 percent of murder trials. We went every month, and I couldn't believe the number of family and friends who came to support us. We had about 60 persons there each time. On his side of the courtroom, he had a couple of friends and two or three family members.

Christmas holidays were approaching and to say that we were not in the Christmas spirit would be an understatement. I found myself starting to guard myself if I had had a few good days in a row. I knew somewhere down the road that I would either see someone who looked like Lisa, or just the thought of Lisa would bring my world down. Believe me, it hurts a lot. What was so difficult was that I couldn't stop it from happening.

Every so often, some of Lisa's friends would call or come by. It was always nice to see them, even though it hurt to think that Lisa should be away at college like they were. Lisa's death affected some of them so that they couldn't cope with being away from home. Some had to transfer back to local colleges. I tried to think that Lisa was away at college. It helped a little. I just pretended that she was away at school.

In September after her death, I started to attend group therapy. We met once a month and it was for family or friends who lost someone they loved through a homicide. This group was more helpful than an earlier group we tried—for anyone who had lost someone they loved. One woman who attended this group had lost her husband to cancer about 10 years earlier. He was in his 70's. But our experience was very different. A young vibrant woman like Lisa does not usually die at the age of 18, especially at the hands of a violent ex-boyfriend. It's still hard to comprehend.

Court was going slowly. Not much was happening with the case. I cannot believe all of the time that is wasted waiting for school records, for blood and hair samples. Like it matters if he had a 4.0 or 2.0 grade point average!

The ex-boyfriend also had to go through psychological tests to prove that he was sane when he murdered Lisa. At one point in the case, he was going to plead guilty if he got less time for the murder. We told the state's attorney that no, we would not accept a plea bargain.

I came home from work one night and Barb told me that she had tried to kill herself. She had come home from visiting Lisa at the cemetery and just wanted to end it all. She sat in the car with the garage door closed and the motor running. It was when the light went out on the automatic timer that she was startled into thinking about what she was trying to do. She decided not to take her life, thank God.

Court was still going on and the end of the trial was nearing. I hoped it wouldn't go to the point that I would have to hear about what happened that night from the ex-boyfriend. In May, 1996, almost two years after Lisa had been murdered, the defense attorney again asked for a plea bargain. The judge said he would give the defendant 75 years in prison. They decided to accept. So did we. He was eligible for the death penalty, but with appeals; I didn't want my family going back to court for another five or seven years. He could have gotten life. But it still wouldn't have brought Lisa back to us. It was time to move on.

Since Lisa's death, I learned a lot more about teen dating violence. I learned about a lot of things I never thought about or even talked about with Lisa or her brother T.J. Truthfully, Lisa was not in an abusive relationship. In the five months that she dated Dan, Lisa was never physically or sexually abused. Maybe somewhat controlled, but then that seems to be common in most relationships. I truly believe Lisa was ready to move on to someone else who had more things in common with her—dancing, laughing, and hanging out with her friends—all of which she was not doing with Dan.

Since Lisa's death, Tom has started his own teen dating violence intervention program. He named it "Dear Lisa" after the series of letters he began writing to his daughter after her death. The program takes Tom across the State of Illinois, and even beyond, to talk to teens about how they might avoid violent dating relationships. He also talks to parents and keeps in close touch with several students through e-mail.

"I am not sure how long I can continue to go to schools and talk about Lisa and dating violence," Tom reports. He sums us his new life's work in a letter that he wrote in his journal. Here is his letter to Lisa:

Dear Lisa,

I am standing in Room M-301, the room you were in as a high school freshman. I'm talking to the freshmen about abuse. Yesterday, I spoke at another high school nearby. God, do I hope I can help just one girl from being abused or, worse yet, 'murdered.' I miss you dearly.

Love,
Daddy

Even though it seldom makes a splash on the nightly news like other forms of violence in which teens engage, teen dating violence can be lethal. Moreover, it can be "invisible." Although Lisa is not here to confirm Tom's impressions, Tom is certain that Lisa would have told him whether there had been any physical or sexual abuse in her relationship with Dan. Then, without Lisa or her parents having any inkling that Dan was unable to accept the dissolution of their relationship, Dan began to stalk Lisa and plan her murder. Only after Dan had beaten Lisa to death did the invisible peril become visible.

Since Lisa's death, Tom has "taken to the road" to talk about teen dating violence. Throughout this time, Tom has received hundreds of letters and e-mails from young men and women involved in violent dating relationships. Some of the letters come from victims. Some come from perpetrators. Most are simply grateful for the advice he gives in his presentations and through e-mail:

- Look for three things in a dating partner: respect, trust, and a sense of humor.
- Recognize the signs of abuse. If you think behaviors are abnormal, they probably are.
- If you think there is a problem, ask for help from a parent, teacher, or friend.
- If you are a friend to a person in an abusive relationship, be nonjudgmental and be there, even if your friend returns to the abuser.

This is advice Alissa could have used when she began to date a young man who would later become her husband, her abuser, and the abusive father of two young boys. Alissa, now separated from her abusive husband after over 20 years of marriage, not only describes the classic characteristics of an abusive relationship—characteristics that are generalized in the following chapter—but also reflects on the way in which abuse can be passed on from one generation to the next. "For the first time, standing on her own two feet," Alissa now worries about the abusive behaviors she sees in her two teenage boys.

Alissa and Sons: Passing on Violence to the Next Generation

I used to stand on my own two feet, but once I met David, all that changed. Dave was athletic, the person in demand. He was known as the person you wanted to be with. He was good looking. He seemed very nice, but I really didn't know him and his family. Although many knew some ugly stuff went on in his home most of his life, I didn't know it mattered. I didn't find out how ugly it could get until we were married.

A friend of mine introduced me to Dave while we were in high school. We all went to this pizza place to get to know each other so we could go to the prom together. But prom night with David was one of the worst nights of my life. . . .

That night, Dave and his friends went to the bathroom to smoke dope. I told him he couldn't do that: 'It's my prom!' And I didn't want to get into trouble.

'It's just one hit,' he said.

Later, the boys dropped us off in front of the restaurant. Their car broke down and they kept us waiting, in the rain, for an hour and a half. We had our fake furs on and our hairdos were a mess. We went to White Castle instead.

He got very drunk at the picnic the next day and was belligerent. So I left with someone else. It was like I belonged to him. 'Nobody leaves me,' he shouted. But I went home with someone else anyway.

We started dating again. The whole time we were dating, he was experimenting with drugs and acid. I used to watch him to make sure he was okay. He was getting way too much into drugs.

I was never scared of him at that point. But everything centered around him.

We went to Florida where we broke up. He wanted to break up because he was playing in a band and he had easy access to other girls, but I was still trying to salvage the relationship. After the breakup someone suggested that I take acid to forget him. It was a bad trip and when I asked him for help, he said, 'You're on your own,' and he wouldn't help me.

I would get so far away when he'd reel me back in and meet me with another girl. Other people didn't want to call me because they were afraid of repercussions with him.

So, I separated myself from him and his friends and went with another guy who was abusive. This one wanted to run my car into a light pole and threatened to blow up the house!

I didn't tell my mother about this latest abuse because I didn't want to worry her. I was petrified, too, that he would hurt my family if I did. And if I told Mother, I'd get lectured to death. So I didn't tell my parents. I could take care of myself, but I didn't want to put them in harm's way. I didn't want to get them involved.

Then this guy threw acid all over my new car. After I told him I wouldn't see him any more, he stole my car.

After that, the threatening phone calls from this guy kept coming. He threatened to set the house on fire. That was the end.

Three years later, out of the blue, Dave called me. His dad was a drunk and there were problems between his parents. We started dating again.

By now, Dave was known for being tough and no one would fight him. He was in a band. He was drinking. I caught a black eye when I tried to break up a fight once.

He wanted to marry me. I told him, 'No drugs or alcohol.' And he was clean and sober an entire year before we married.

I don't know what I said or did, but one day about a month before we were married, he came up behind me and slapped me across the head from behind. He knocked me straight off the chair.

I told him that I couldn't deal with this. And he got very contrite. He promised me that this would never happen to me again. He said he didn't know what came over him.

Nothing ever happened again while we were dating. Nope. But it started the week after we were married. From the point that I walked into the house we had bought, it just began. I had walked into hell.

We would get invited out and he'd say we couldn't go. He'd be pushing or shoving or flipping tables. He was big on coming right up into my face and yelling and telling me that I should understand what he was capable of doing to me.

Dave would get very drunk and say things that were embarrassing or hurtful to our hosts. I lived in terror of what he would say to people.

We'd get calls from his mother because his father was being very abusive to her. And then the sons would go over to his parents' home and beat the shit out of their father. This was the first time I actually learned what his family life had been like.

Why didn't I leave? I had become agoraphobic. I couldn't leave my own house. God was punishing me because I couldn't even live in my own house now, and I couldn't leave it either.

Then, after five years, I got pregnant. He came home one night while I was in the early stages of my pregnancy. He was very drunk and was just raunchy. He started pushing me around. I couldn't deal with this because I was pregnant. I'd be on the floor and he'd be kicking me. I'd be cradling the baby and he'd be kicking me in the back. It was then that I confronted his mother about what had been happening. She was shocked to hear this since she thought that Dave would never be abusive because of all that he had seen his father do to her. She made him promise to stop and, for a while, he did. But I started thinking about divorce.

But then, just as I'd think about leaving, things would get better. He'd go out and buy a new car. Financially, though, there was no way I could leave him and my mother was no help. She'd say, 'Well, at least you're getting a paycheck.'

One day, I literally had to lock myself in a room. What was I doing to deserve this? Why wasn't I a stronger person to pull myself up by my bootstraps and get out of there? But my family couldn't understand panic and agoraphobia, so how could they understand this?

When I asked for help, Mother again insisted, 'You have to work this out for yourselves.' She heard Dave say that he was going to kill me, and she told us to handle it ourselves. So why would she help? It was one tangled ball. Even after the kids were born, Dave would take them out in the car when he was drunk. I couldn't find them. But my mother would never get involved, even though she knew everything. She'd just say, 'You have to work out your own problems.'

I couldn't go outside the house, but Dave had his circle of friends and family that he went out drinking with. I had no friends except Sharon. And I didn't tell her because she didn't understand what was wrong with me. You have somebody who is telling you that you are crazy, so how many people do you want to know you are crazy? Actually, I prayed to be insane, but the psychologist said I was not. But if I were insane, then I'd be at peace. Finally, I found a therapist who would talk to me over the phone. I couldn't go out of the house. I thought there was something wrong with me. Dave used that to his advantage. 'Yes, you are crazy,' he'd tell me.

Then he totalled six cars. Each time, he was drunk.

When I was in the delivery room waiting to deliver Kevin, he told me that he was trying to decide whether we should stay together. He liked it when I breastfed Kevin because it absolved him from having anything to do with the baby. Kevin served as a barrier between him and me. I liked breastfeeding because it was the only time I ever felt completely relaxed. It was a closeness that I had never felt before, even when I was pregnant.

The abuse became so bad that when my two kids became teens, they were telling me to get him out of the house. He would go after the two boys with such force, you'd be afraid he wouldn't stop. I'd have to punch and kick him to get him off the kids. I was the physical barrier between him and the kids. Then the kids started to become unruly. Now I couldn't discipline them. I became verbally abusive to them because they listened to Dave when he was that way with them.

Dave used to boast to our kids that when he was 16, he was the 'toughest kid walking.' 'No one will ever mess with me,' he'd say. Dave's family idolized him. 'He's the baddest mf-er in the world,' they'd boast.

Every time he was drunk, he would boast about his athletic ability. No family member could ever excel in athletics, not even his children. The kids actually preferred it when Dave was drunk. It was the only time he would talk to them.

Dave never showed any affection toward me unless he was drunk. No holding hands. No nothing like that. And if you got sick, he wanted nothing to do with you.

Then I did get sick. I had difficulty swallowing, and I'd have to go out to have medical tests. Pretty tough for an agoraphobic. After agreeing to take medication to ease the panic I was experiencing, I was able to leave the house and even have friends again. The more I was able to leave the house, the more verbally abusive he became. Up until the day he left, he was determined to convince me I was crazy. He told me all my troubles were a 'figment of my imagination' and that to get set straight, I should just 'have the shit knocked out of me.'

By now, I was able to get out of the house. I got a job, and had my own insurance. I could stand up to him. And the occasion for me to stand up for myself soon came.

One night, he didn't want me to do something. He cracked me so hard his handprint was still on my face. My friend was a detective and asked him why he did this to me. 'Why, Dave?'

'Yeah, I did it. She deserved it,' Dave boasted.

'But nobody deserves this, Dave,' I thought. ' Nobody.'

I began to play cards regularly with friends. I had a place where I could go and not feel like I was crazy.

Two years later, he beat me black and blue all over. It was Mother's Day. 'Please make a police report,' my friends told me. 'They'll come and arrest him.' But I couldn't have him arrested in front of the kids.

We finally decided to separate. I planned to move out. The day before I moved out, Dave went berserk when he found out that I discovered money he had been keeping from me. That day was completely brutal, and I will never forget it. He had me cornered. I couldn't get to a phone. He had me by the hair and was trying to pull it off and scalp me. I flew into walls. Then it was a blur. I tried to fight him off for my life. I knew I should have had an 'out' but that day, I was tired of dealing with all of it. For the first time, I didn't care.

How would he explain my condition when I told what he had done to me? Dave just told me that he'd just tell anyone who wondered why I looked the way I did was that I tried to hurt myself. 'Nobody's gonna believe you now. That's just what you needed.'

As I tell you this story today, I am 49 years old.

Now my concern is for the boys.

Alissa's story illustrates how Dave fits the classic profile of an abuser. He is manipulative and has convinced Alissa that she is crazy and to blame for all their problems. He has made Alissa question her own good instincts by convincing her that she deserves the brutality and abuse he has inflicted on her. Further, Dave exercises control and power over Alissa through physical intimidation and actual violence such as slapping, kicking, yelling, and punching. This abuse becomes worse when she becomes pregnant, and Alissa is forced to shield not only herself but also her unborn baby.

Not only does Alissa's story illustrate the profile of an abuser, but also it illustrates the cycle of abuse: Violent incidents are followed by an abuser's apologies and promises to reform. For some period, a "normal" relationship seems to follow. Then, usually without warning, the abuser becomes violent again. This time, however, the violence is even more brutal than before. Maggie also experienced this cycle of abuse, apology, and return to "normalcy," followed again by more abuse in her relationship with Mark.

For victims or survivors such as Alissa, the abuse begins with disbelief and confusion. Alissa was stunned at Dave's behavior. It was apparently unprovoked and came from nowhere. What had caused Dave to slap her? What had *she* done to cause Dave to slap her?

Like Maggie, Alissa now faced the question of whether Dave's behavior was a "moment or a movement." Did he just lose control for that one instant, or was a pattern of behavior beginning to develop?

After many years of abuse, both before and after marriage, Alissa came to the same conclusion as Maggie: Dave was a violent abusive person, and nothing Alissa could do could change Dave. Alissa would have to change herself. However, where could she go for help?

Unlike Maggie, Alissa had no sympathetic parents to turn to once she became aware of the seriousness of her situation. Moreover, Alissa had two children to care for and to protect. She was not financially independent so she could not provide for her children on her own. Maggie, by contrast, had not married her abusive boyfriend. She did not have children and, because she was still in college, was carried on her parents' health insurance. The absence of health insurance was, according to Alissa, one of the major factors that kept her tied to her abusive spouse. Moreover, Maggie's parents were helpful when she decided to separate from Mark. Alissa's parents were not. Alissa was isolated and alone.

Maggie related that while she was dating Mark, she began to isolate herself from her friends. Indeed, some of Maggie's friends began to withdraw because of Mark's erratic behavior. The isolation that Alissa experienced was also characteristic of her abusive relationship. Dave tried to convince Alissa that she was crazy and, to some degree, it worked. Moreover, Alissa's parents were unsympathetic to her situation. Thus, there was no possible support from them. Initially, because of Dave's controlling behavior, he and Alissa would not go out except on Dave's terms. Later in the relationship, no one wanted to socialize with Dave and Alissa because Dave's drinking and abusive behaviors were unpredictable, if not terrifying. Alissa herself was embarrassed to go out with Dave because she could never count on him to remain civil toward her or toward others. Her sense of isolation intensified.

Maggie and Alissa are alike insofar as both were able to separate from abusive relationships. While such separations occurred at different ages and under different circumstances, Alissa is also able to share the story of how children who see abuse in parents can themselves sometimes become abusive.

A synthesis of the stories of hundreds of young women and adults such as Maggie, Lisa, and Alissa, Chapter Two presents a general profile of the invisible peril. This chapter illustrates that the abuse young teenage women experience in their dating relationships very much parallels the experiences of adult women in abusive relationships. As Chapter Three subsequently illustrates, however, the resources young teenage women have at their disposal to assist them in separating from abusive relationships are quite different from the varied resources available to adult women seeking to end an abusive relationship.

CHAPTER 2

A PROFILE OF THE
INVISIBLE PERIL

"Well, I sure don't like it when he shows up all the time wherever I am. Even when I don't tell him where I am going, he's there. It's like he's got radar or something."

"He" is a 26-year-old man and dating partner of a 16-year-old African American high school junior who had just asked me to explain what stalking is. After I explained to her that stalking was repeatedly following or harassing a person so that the person feels threatened or unsafe, she asked me, "Do you think that's abuse?"

I turned the question back to her. "How do you feel when it happens?"

"Well," she replied, "I sure don't like it. And it's scary too. But he loves me or he wouldn't want to be with me all the time, would he? Isn't that why he follows me everywhere?"

Teen Dating Violence: It Is Not about Love

If being followed everywhere is unwelcome by the one being pursued, however, then the behavior becomes stalking, and stalking is not about love. Rather, it is about jealousy run amok. It is about being harassed. It is about being manipulated. It is about feeling scared.

Stalking, like other forms of dating violence, is about the exercise of power and control over another who does not welcome such control. For a teenage woman, it manifests itself in demands to "check in" with her boyfriend so he knows where she is and with whom she is at all times. It is about a young woman's feeling uncomfortable or angry when her boyfriend unexpectedly appears and tries to pull her away from what she is doing with her friends. It is about isolation and mistrust. At worst, it is about the fear that a teenage woman feels when she has been physically threatened or harmed by a boyfriend who just won't leave her alone.

Even if a boyfriend does not follow up on his threats, stalking is abusive. It is emotionally and psychologically abusive. While stalking is a behavior that often confuses young women, like many other forms of dating behavior, it is not about love. It is about abuse. Moreover, it is against the law.

The 16-year-old woman who was uncomfortable with being followed all the time had good instincts. She did not like her boyfriend's behavior. She resented it, and she was even scared by it. However, as with many young women who lack life experience and self-esteem, her good instincts gave way to self-doubt and rationalization.

How could the attention he shows me by showing up wherever I am be something to be worried about, much less abusive? How can I tell him that I want some space from him when we love each other so much? And isn't love about wanting to be together to share both the good and the bad times? Perhaps I am just being too sensitive. How can love be abusive or violent?

These comments suggest that this young woman is now very confused about what is happening in her dating relationship. Just when she starts to pay attention to the vague discomfort that something is wrong in her dating relationship, she doubts herself and rationalizes her boyfriend's behavior. She begins to confuse control and abuse with love and care. Without a significant change in her perspective and without behavioral change on his part, the teenage woman immerses herself in a dating relationship that can easily escalate into physical violence or murder.

Because a teenage woman lacks the life experience of an adult, she sometimes tolerates behaviors that are either inappropriate or patently abusive. Unfortunately, she does not usually know that she is not alone in her confusion, or even in her dating experiences.

Research suggests that about 5 percent of all women will experience stalking at least once during their lives.[1] In fact, because stalking poses a particularly dangerous physical threat to women, the California State Assembly became the first to pass an anti-stalking statute in 1990.

In California, those who can be prosecuted for stalking include "any person who willfully, maliciously, and repeatedly follows or harasses another person and who makes a credible threat with the intent to place that person in reasonable fear for his or her safety—or the safety of his or her immediate family."[2] For stalking to occur, therefore, it is not necessary that the stalker carry out his or her threat. Rather, repeated acts that annoy, torment, or terrorize a woman, even over a relatively short period of time, may constitute a credible threat. According to the State of California, stalking constitutes a credible threat because it places a young woman, a teenager under the age of 18, in fear for her safety. Thus, a teenager who senses that something is just "not right" in her relationship would be well advised to think of her boyfriend's behavior as stalking. Then, she should think of the dangers that stalking poses.

Besides stalking, what other forms does teen dating violence take? What behaviors and patterns characterize it? What is the profile of an abuser, and how can a teenage woman determine whether the violence is escalating, even to the point of a lethal outcome?

Legal Definitions

The best descriptions of the variety of forms that teen dating violence takes may be found in domestic violence statutes and in the literature provided by domestic violence counselors, court advocates, law enforcement officers, and private and government social service agencies. As a relatively comprehensive statute, for example, the *Illinois Domestic Violence Act of 1986* provides a list of the most common forms of intimate partner abuse, whether it occurs between adults or between adults and minors. Specifically, the statute characterizes domestic violence as physical abuse, harassment, intimidation, interference with one's personal liberty, or willful deprivation.[3] Similar to statutes in other states, the Illinois act further specifies that domestic violence includes situations in which the perpetrator's actions cause emotional distress for the victim. Examples of such behavior are stalking or unwanted repeated telephone calls; the threat of physical force or its actual use to confine, restrain, or intimidate the victim; the immediate risk of physical harm; or sexual abuse that forces the victim to engage in sexual acts against her will.[4]

The Marquette County Michigan Law Enforcement Domestic Violence Policy and Procedures document states that domestic violence occurs "when a person by means of force or violence causes, or attempts to cause, harm to another family or household members. This may include, but is not limited to, bodily injury (assault and battery) [and] fear of imminent bodily injury (assault)."[5] Thus, policies that redress domestic violence and its subcategory of teen dating violence vary from state to state. However, there are a number of common elements in the definitions in these statutes that describe abuse between intimate partners, whether between adults or teens:

- Intimate partner violence occurs between people in close, personal, familial, or sexual relationships.

- Intimate partner violence can occur between heterosexual or homosexual couples.

- The perpetrator of violence can be either a male or a female.

- The victim can be either a male or a female.

- Intimate partner violence can be actual or threatened.

- The form that intimate partner violence takes can be emotional/psychological, physical, or sexual abuse, although only a few states specifically identify emotional/psychological abuse as a form of intimate partner violence.

In addition to these similarities, the causes, the characteristics, and the behavioral profile of an abuser in a teen dating relationship are similar to the causes, characteristics, and behavioral profiles of abusers involved in domestic violence. Similarly, the cycle of abuse that describes domestic violence also describes teen dating violence.

The Causes of Teen Dating Violence

As with domestic violence, attitudes about women's proper societal roles and men's issues about power and control are usually the root causes of most teen dating violence. Couple jealousy, insecurity, and the "lack of [a] social stigma attached to using violence to obtain a desired objective,"[6] with a male's need to control and dominate women, and the foundation for intimate partner abuse has been laid. Such domination, often reinforced by images in the media, may justify using physically aggressive behavior.

An abusive man wants to control the way in which his partner dresses, with whom she associates, and the way that she behaves with him and with others. Further, as a master manipulator, an abusive man will try to exercise psychological control over his partner. He will humiliate her in front of others and he may threaten to harm her. Sometimes, he will even threaten to harm himself. He may actually harm himself, but not usually until after he has harmed his partner first.

Because he is typically physically stronger than a woman, a man is able to "enforce" his demands on his partner through the exercise of physical force. Moreover, because he probably has a need to exert power and control over his partner, he will use the fact that his female partner has denied him something, usually sexual, to justify his anger.

On the female side of the relationship, one may wonder why a teenage woman might become involved with an abusive male in the first place. Like the man who may abuse her, a teenage woman may also model the behaviors around her, especially those she sees in her family, in social settings, or in the media. While she will certainly see images of strong, independent, caring, and lovable women involved in healthy relationships with men, she will also see women who are submissive to males in intimate partner relationships. Further, a teenage woman may feel that she should "stand by her man," regardless of the cost to herself, and that she should always be ready to subordinate her own needs and desires, whether for independence or for other personal relationships, to the needs of her male dating partner.

As she begins to devote her life totally to her boyfriend, she also begins to isolate herself from others, especially those, typically adults, who might provide another perspective on the healthiness of her dating relationship. In the best circumstances, these adults could point out that her boyfriend's behavior is neither common nor appropriate. Further, they could help bolster her self-esteem, not by dismissing her concerns and her passionate intensity as "growing pains" or as "puppy love," but by helping her see her boyfriend's behavior for what it is: the inappropriate exercise of power and control.

However, as discussed later in Chapter Seven, a teenage woman does not find many reasons to talk to adults about problems she encounters while dating. Some of these reasons are related to adults' behaviors and attitudes, but others are related to the penchant a teenage woman may have for holding herself totally accountable for her boyfriend's behavior. Because she views herself as responsible for his behavior, she often reacts by trying to "manage" the situation herself. Unfortunately, such management usually comes with a type of self-chastisement that reinforces the young woman's belief that she is responsible for provoking her boyfriend's violent outbursts or sexual assault.

Thus, the causes of teen dating violence are twofold. The first is found in the abuser's distorted idea that he has the right to control how others, especially his dating partner, responds to him. The second is found in the limited life experience of the victim and in her reluctance to confide in others. Together, these factors make a teenage woman vulnerable and likely to tolerate some forms of abuse more than her adult counterparts.

The Characteristics of Teen Dating Violence

Not only are the causes of teen dating violence similar to those of domestic violence but also the results of teen dating violence mirror "adult domestic violence in that it exists on a continuum ranging from emotional and verbal abuse to rape and murder."[7] To help teenage women who are confused about what they are experiencing in their dating relationships, domestic violence counselors, women's advocates, police departments, and social service agencies have identified a number of signs that suggest when a dating relationship has become abusive. For example, the Domestic Abuse Intervention Project of Duluth, Minnesota, has compiled a checklist of signs of emotional, physical, and sexual abuse. Based on this organization's "Power and Control and Equality Wheels," I largely quote, and use with permission, these materials. However, I have adapted them to distinguish between young teenage women living at home and those few teens living with their abusive partners.[8]

SIGNS OF EMOTIONAL ABUSE

The following behaviors generally characterize a dating partner who is emotionally or psychologically abusive: An abusive personality will be guilty of . . .

- Putting his partner down;
- Making his partner feel bad about herself;
- Calling his partner names;
- Making his partner think she is crazy;
- Playing mind games with his partner;
- Controlling what his partner does;
- Controlling whom his partner sees;
- Controlling whom his partner talks to;
- Controlling where his partner goes;
- Threatening to kill his partner;
- Treating his partner like a servant;
- Making all the "big" decisions;
- Acting like the "master of the castle";
- Putting his partner in fear by using looks, actions, gestures, or a loud voice, or by smashing things or destroying her property.

SIGNS OF PHYSICAL ABUSE

The following behaviors generally profile a dating partner who is physically abusive. Typically, he engages in . . .

- Pushing;
- Shoving;
- Hitting;

- Slapping;
- Choking;
- Pulling hair;
- Punching;
- Kicking;
- Grabbing;
- Using a weapon;
- Beating;
- Throwing down;
- Twisting arms;
- Tripping;
- Biting.

SIGNS OF SEXUAL ABUSE

The following behaviors generally characterize a dating partner who is abusing his partner sexually. He will . . .

- Make his partner do sexual things against her will;
- Physically attack the sexual parts of his partner's body;
- Treat his partner like a sex object.

SIGNS OF ABUSE BETWEEN PARTNERS LIVING TOGETHER OR HAVING A CHILD TOGETHER

Also abusive, but more characteristic of the situation of a teenage woman who lives with her partner, or has a child by him, are the following behaviors of the teen's abuser:

- Trying to keep his partner from getting or keeping a job;
- Making his partner ask for money;
- Giving his partner an allowance;
- Taking his partner's money;
- Making her feel guilty about the child/children;
- Using the child/children to give messages to his partner;
- Threatening to take the child/children away from his partner;
- Reporting his partner to child welfare.[9]

(Minnesota Program Development, Inc. Used with permission.)

The Profile of Potential Abusers

Regardless of whether the victim is an adult or a young teenager, the characteristics and profile of an abusive relationship are similar. The Project for Victims of Family Violence, Inc., in Fayetteville, Arkansas, in their widely quoted pamphlet *Signs to Look for in a Battering Personality*, describes this profile. Used here with permission, the Project identifies the following 17 characteristics:[10]

1. BEING JEALOUS

At the beginning of a relationship, an abuser will say that jealousy is a sign of love. It is not. It is a sign of possessiveness and of a lack of trust. The potential abuser will not only question to whom the woman talks but also accuse her of flirting with others. He will be jealous of the time she spends with friends or family, or of virtually any time she spends away from him or out of his control. He may even exhibit strange behaviors such as checking her mileage or asking friends to watch her.

2. CONTROLLING BEHAVIOR

At first, the abuser will say that his controlling behavior is for the safety of the woman so that she will make good decisions for herself. It is not. It is about controlling whom she meets, where she goes, how she dresses, and how she makes personal decisions.

3. WANTING QUICK INVOLVEMENT

The abuser comes on like a whirlwind, claiming, "I've never felt loved like this by anyone." He will then pressure the woman to commit to the relationship in such a way that later, the woman may feel guilty about wanting to slow down or break off the involvement.

4. HAVING UNREALISTIC EXPECTATIONS

The abuser expects his partner to meet all his needs. She is supposed to take care of everything for him emotionally.

5. ISOLATING HIS PARTNER

The abuser tries to cut off his partner from all resources. If she has men friends, then he tells her that she is a "whore." If she has women friends, then she is a lesbian. If she's close to the family, then she is "tied to the apron strings." Besides attacking her supporters, the abuser also accuses her friends of causing trouble.

6. BLAMING OTHERS FOR PROBLEMS

Someone is always doing wrong to the abuser or someone is always out to get him. When he makes mistakes, he blames his partner for upsetting him. His partner is supposedly at fault for all that goes wrong.

7. BLAMING OTHERS FOR FEELINGS

He will tell his partner that she is responsible for his feelings; for example, he may say "you make me mad." But she does not make him "mad." Rather, he is using his feelings to manipulate her.

8. BEING HYPERSENSITIVE

An abuser is easily insulted. He takes the slightest setbacks as personal attacks. He will rant and rave about the injustice of things that have happened to him. For the most part, the "things" that send him into a rage are not even setbacks but just part of daily living, for example, being asked to work overtime or to do chores.

9. DISPLAYING CRUELTY TO ANIMALS OR CHILDREN

The abuser punishes animals brutally or is insensitive to their pain or suffering. He may expect others, especially children, to do things beyond their capabilities.

10. INSISTING ON THE "PLAYFUL" USE OF FORCE IN SEX

The abuser may like to throw his partner down and hold her down during sex. He may want to act out fantasies where she is helpless. He lets his partner know that the idea of rape is exciting.

11. BEING VERBALLY ABUSIVE

In addition to saying things that are meant to be cruel and hurtful, the abuser degrades his partner, curses her, or runs down her accomplishments. The abuser will tell his partner that she is stupid and unable to function without him.

12. INSISTING ON RIGID SEX ROLES

The abuser expects his partner to serve him. He may insist that she stay at home and obey him in all things. The abuser views his partner as inferior to him, as inferior to men in general. He believes that she should only be responsible for menial tasks. He tells her that she is unable to be a whole person without him.

13. EVIDENCING DR. JEKYLL AND MR. HYDE PERSONALITY CHANGES

The abuser confuses his partner because of his sudden changes in mood. Because of his erratic behavior—enraged one minute and nice the next—she may think he has a mental problem. Explosiveness and moodiness are typical of people who beat their partners.

14. EVIDENCING PAST BATTERING

The abuser may say he has hit women in the past, but he will say that they made him do it. His partners did not make him violent. Situations do not make a person an abusive personality, nor does anything a woman says justify her partner's physical abuse.

15. THREATENING VIOLENCE

The abuser uses threats of physical force, for example, telling his partner, "I'll slap you in the mouth," or "I'll kill you," or "I'll break your neck." An abuser will try to excuse these threats by saying, "Everybody talks like that." However, this statement is not true. Most people do not threaten to kill their mates or partners.

16. BREAKING OR STRIKING OBJECTS

By breaking things like beloved possessions of his partner, or by beating the table with his fist, the abuser terrorizes his partner into submission. Breaking or striking objects is not only a sign of emotional immaturity but also a sign of great danger. Further, it suggests that he thinks he has the "right" to punish or frighten his partner.

17. USING ANY FORCE DURING AN ARGUMENT

Here, an abuser may hold his partner down, physically restrain her from leaving the room, or push or shove her. He may hold his partner against the wall and say, "You are going to listen to me!"[11]

(Project for Victims of Family Violence, Inc. Used with permission.)

Signs of Escalating Violence and Potentially Lethal Outcomes

Once a young teenage woman has recognized these behaviors in her dating relationship and has acknowledged that her partner is abusing her, she then needs to assess whether she is in a potentially lethal situation. The South Suburban Family Shelter, Inc., in Homewood, Illinois, has developed a scale where abusive behaviors are listed in order of severity.[12] In increasing order of severity, these behaviors include the following:

1. Throwing things, punching the wall;
2. Pushing, shoving, grabbing, throwing things at the victim;

3. Slapping with an open hand;

4. Kicking, biting;

5. Hitting with closed fists;

6. Attempting to strangle;

7. Beating (pinned to wall/floor, repeated kicks, punches);

8. Threatening with a weapon;

9. Assaulting with a weapon.[13]

To this list, Hart (1992) adds 11 other behaviors that suggest that the violence between intimate partners may be escalating to lethal proportions.[14] In particular, she proposes that women should be especially wary when their partners do the following:

10. Make threats of homicide or suicide;

11. Describe fantasies of homicide or suicide;

12. Become acutely depressed;

13. Possess weapons;

14. Report that they "can't live without them";

15. Tell their partners that they have lost hope for a positive future without them;

16. Become enraged when they believe their victims are leaving;

17. Consume alcohol or use drugs when despairing or enraged;

18. Abuse or mutilate pets;

19. Have access to their partner's person or family members;

20. Take hostages.[15]

Such behaviors depict what each teenage woman should look for in the behavior of her male partner to assess the onset of imminent and increasing violence. However, each teenage woman should also know that a dating relationship that has already exhibited violence can turn deadly when *she* behaves in a different way or when *her* circumstances change.

For example, violence is likely to escalate when a teenage woman becomes pregnant. Abuse is also likely to worsen when the abuser perceives that the relationship may be at risk of ending, either because she has told the abuser that she "wants out," or because she "has gone public" to her parents, or even to the police, about her abuse. Perhaps the young woman has even gone as far as to request and receive an order of protection from the courts.

In each of these circumstances, research suggests that the potential for the rapid escalation of violence is substantial. Stark and Flitcraft (1988), for example, report that 75 percent of battered women seeking emergency medical services may do so after separation from their partner.[16] While these statistics do not differentiate between the experience of teenage women and adults, they nevertheless illustrate the dangers young women might encounter in trying to separate from abusive partners.

The Cycle of Teen Dating Violence

One of the characteristics of teen dating violence that is most confusing to a teenage woman is that the abuse occurs in cycles. There are good times, and there are bad times. These times, though, are cyclical and fairly predictable.

In the first sequence of the cycle of abuse, the love the dating partners experience for each other is very romantic and very intense. During this period of infatuation, the boyfriend may seem to be everything the young teenage woman ever wanted in a dating partner, or even in a lifelong partner. He is solicitous. He is sensitive. He is respectful. He may bring her thoughtful gifts or write wonderful letters.

For her part, the young woman is delighted. She responds to her partner's overtures with equal sensitivity, care, and concern. She supports her boyfriend in his activities. She awaits his calls anxiously, and she is excited about being seen with him. She is also relieved to have found a dating partner. Because she has a boyfriend, the social stigma of being without a boyfriend has ended. There is someone who loves her. She will not die an old maid.

For their part, parents may know little or nothing about their daughter's boyfriend. Alternatively, they may only know what their daughter tells them: that he is wonderful and accomplished, and that she is lucky to have found such a prize. Without information to the contrary, all of this is reassuring—perhaps too reassuring. However, it is hard to tell whether there is trouble because teen dating partners, whether "Prince Charmings" or potential abusers, can look pretty much the same in the early stages of a dating relationship. This is also one of the reasons why the second stage of an abusive relationship—the stage when a partner suddenly explodes—comes as a shock to so many young teenage women. Consider the following situation.

After several dates, all has been going well. Suddenly, something happens. According to many young women, their partners just suddenly explode or become enraged for apparently little or no reason. Often, the boyfriend's rage will have been preceded by drinking or drug use, but not always. Sometimes, it is sparked by the jealousy the boyfriend feels when he sees his girlfriend in the company of others, especially other males.

Suddenly, I found myself pinned against the wall with his hands around my throat. I didn't even know how I got there. He just kept pushing me into the wall telling me never to embarrass him that way again. I was stunned. This had never happened before. Then he hit me. How could he hit me? I just went blank. I wanted to get away, but he was too strong for me. He just kept screaming in my face and threatening me. 'Never, ever do that to me again,' he screamed repeatedly while pinning me to the wall. So I promised never to do it again, even though I didn't even know what 'it' was. I was just talking to my friends, but I guess I wasn't giving him enough attention. What else could I have done to make him so angry with me?

In the second stage of the cycle of abuse, mistrust deteriorates into anger and rage. Rage leads to physical violence. The physical violence, so unexpected and out of character with prior behaviors, stuns the victim. Perhaps sexual abuse ensues. To escape from the immediate threat of additional violence or even death, the young victim may promise to do whatever her partner tells her to do. Later, she rationalizes the violent outbreak and wonders what she could have done to make her boyfriend so angry.

In contrast, the boyfriend often becomes quite contrite and later tries to explain his behavior. His contrition and remorse signal the third stage of the cycle of abuse.

I was just out of control. I don't know what happened to me, but when I saw you with Gary I just went ballistic. Don't do that to me. Please. I love you so much. I just can't stand seeing you with another guy. I promise I'll never hurt you again. Won't you forgive me? I love you so much. Honest. I will never do that again. Can you ever forgive me?

In the third stage of the cycle of abuse, the abuser can be truly remorseful. He seems honestly to believe that he will not repeat his abusive behavior. Such remorse is one of the reasons he is so convincing to his young partner. Moreover, because she is so stunned and the incident seems so out of character with her partner's prior behaviors, the young woman typically forgives him for just "having had a bad day."

Unfortunately, her dating partner will not usually be able to keep his promise not to explode again. Rather, after a period when there is less tension, or even when things seem "back to normal," something again happens that throws the boyfriend into a rage. This time, however, the violence is even more brutal than the first time.

As Wells notes, these three stages of the cycle of abuse can be summarized as follows:[17]

STAGE ONE: TENSION BUILDING

- Minor battering incidents become more frequent.
- The young teenage woman believes she has some control of the situation and that by calming her boyfriend, she can prevent his anger from escalating.
- Battering behavior has been consciously measured by the abuser.

STAGE TWO: ACUTE BATTERING

- There is a lack of control by abuser.
- The couple acknowledges the serious nature of the incident.
- There is a lack of predictability in the relationship.
- The young woman feels trapped, unable to flee.
- The young woman feels shock, denial, disbelief.
- Police help is requested.

STAGE THREE: KINDNESS AND CONTRITION

- The abuser is charming, loving, and begs her for forgiveness.
- The young woman believes this is what her boyfriend is really like.
- The young woman believes the abuser will get the help he needs if she stays, and that he will harm himself if she leaves.
- If the young woman has filed charges, then she may drop them during this phase.[18]

Once is usually not enough for an abuser when a teen dating relationship takes a violent turn. The abuser wants to exert increasing levels of control and power over his young partner, and so the level of violence escalates each time and at each stage. The cycle of abuse is repeated until the young victim takes steps to extricate herself from the situation, the abuser gets help, the court intervenes, or someone—usually the female partner—is murdered.

Teen dating violence mirrors domestic violence in its causes, in its characteristics, and in its effects. Given the nature of the police responses to this problem, it would seem that young teenage women might also have the same access to legal remedies and resources as do adult women. Such is not the case, however. As Chapter Three illustrates, the problem of teen dating violence cannot be successfully addressed by most current policies, laws, and programs that have been designed to solve the problems of adults involved in domestic violence situations. At best, a one-size-fits-all policy approach to intimate partner violence is ineffective. At worst, such an approach can delude us into thinking that society is being responsive to the particular set of problems that young teenage women face in violent dating relationships, when, in fact, it is not.

CHAPTER 3

CURRENT TEEN DATING VIOLENCE POLICY: INEFFECTIVE AND WITH HARMFUL EFFECTS

Re-key your locks. Install deadbolts on all outside doors. Change your phone number to an unlisted number. Move to a temporary safe house or shelter. Set up code words with friends or neighbors to signal the onset of violence. Call the police. Get an order of protection or a temporary restraining order.

These are strategies that domestic violence counselors and court advocates typically suggest to women who want to get out of a violent intimate partner relationship. As helpful as these strategies might be, however, they are more appropriate to adult women in abusive relationships than to teenage women who experience violence in their dating relationships. How realistic is it, for example, for a teenage woman who wants to separate from a violent dating relationship to move away from home? To change her name? To change the locks or the phone number at the family home? To open and keep a substantial bank account? To stop going to school? To devise an escape plan? To call the police? Or to apply for an order of protection?

The advice that the Domestic Violence Unit of the San Diego Police Department gives to women in abusive situations is similar to the advice proffered by domestic violence counselors and court advocates. This advice, however, while appropriate and actionable for adults, is probably not very realistic for most teens trying to separate from abusive partners. Consider the extent to which teenage women might be able to follow the strategies, especially without her parents' knowledge, that the San Diego Domestic Violence Unit advocates.

"If you are a victim of domestic violence, and a police report is filed, you should consider the following alternatives which will be critical for your safety:

- Consider keeping an emergency bag packed with clothing, money, emergency telephone numbers and/or toys for children.

- Home security is extremely important. Each door and window should always be LOCKED, whether you are at home or away for a period of time.

- If you have obtained a restraining order, it is preferred that you re-key your locks.

- Install dead bolts on all outside doors. Place a dowel in sliding glass doors and windows.

- While at home, never automatically open the door after the first knock.

- Install adequate lighting outside.

- Change your phone number to a new UNLISTED number if possible."[1]

How is it that such strategies are proposed to all victims of domestic violence when it is so difficult for teens to adopt them?

Because teen dating violence mirrors intimate partner abuse among adults in its causes, characteristics, and effects, it seems that policy makers mistakenly infer that the remedies that are effective for adults are also effective for young teenage women. In reality, however, the experience of teens involved in intimate partner abuse is very different from that of adults. In particular, teens and adults differ in emotional and developmental levels. There are legal and circumstantial differences between teens and adults, and they have different abilities to access social and health care services.

Differences in Emotional and Developmental Levels

"The developmental aspects of adolescence differentiate teen dating violence from abuse in adult relationships."[2] Compared to most adults, teens have fewer life experiences to serve as frames of reference against which to evaluate their own behaviors or the behaviors of others. Also in comparison to adults, they have relatively limited dating experience. Because they have little context against which to evaluate what they are experiencing, the lines between playful and abusive teasing, harmless and painful tickling, and rough-housing and assault are confusing. This confusion can lead to the toleration of abusive behavior that should be rejected out-of-hand as disrespectful and inappropriate.

Should a young teenage woman become involved in an abusive dating relationship, she is as likely as an adult woman to become isolated or to withdraw from friends. However, a teen's isolation may be even greater than that of an adult because the teen is mistrustful of adults and badly wants to establish her independence from them. Moreover, a teen is often afraid to confide in others for fear of being punished for a situation she did not create.

While adult women in abusive relationships may be isolated from family and peers by their abusers, and while they also may fear reprisals for "telling tales outside the family," they do not generally mistrust all adults. In addition, they do not usually fear punishment from those in whom they confide. Thus, adults in abusive situations may be more inclined to seek out or accept advice from other adults. Teens, by contrast, will generally have a more limited social network of possible helpers to whom they can turn and, for a number of reasons that I will discuss later, are reticent to seek such help.

When teens do talk, however, they prefer to talk with one of their peers. Unfortunately, peers are often as naïve about dating violence as are the victims themselves. Thus, while peers may provide a compassionate ear and become a kind of sounding board for a dating violence victim, they do not typically have any more wisdom or life experience to share than the victim herself.

The early years of womanhood are formative. They are often characterized by emotional volatility, dramatic physical and psychological change, and a burning desire to separate oneself from one's parents while linking inextricably to one's peers. Moreover, most young teenage women do not want to stand out from their peers, especially in the ways that they relate to the opposite sex. For teens, the need to fit in with one's peers is paramount, even to the point of making lifestyle choices, choices in friends, or choices of dating partners, that are self-destructive. Sousa (1999) becomes quite specific:

> To cope with stress and gain status with their peers, many adolescents also rush to become involved in intimate relationships. Some accept abuse as part of those relationships. . . . The social demands of adolescence often require that a young woman have a boyfriend . . . [and] the norms of adolescent peer groups often support stereotypical behaviors: dominance for men and passivity for women. . . . Girls are expected to be supportive and are responsible for the success or failure of the relationship. Boys are expected to be sexually forceful, to exhibit aggressive behavior, and to be in control of the decisions in the relationship. These stereotypes are often superimposed on an intense level of feeling. A teenager may view possessive jealousy and controlling behavior as loving devotion and may confuse the perpetrator's remorse with intimacy.[3]

Legal and Circumstantial Differences between Adults and Teens

While there are some important variations from state to state, most domestic or "family" violence laws apply only to those who are living with their abusers, those who have had a child with the abuser, or those who have been legally emancipated by the courts. Each of these conditions is easier to meet if the person suffering the abuse is an adult or if the teen has the support of her parents while she tries to negotiate the complexities of a legal system that focuses more on the circumstances of adults than on teens.

NOT LIVING WITH THE ABUSER

Teenage women involved in dating violence do not typically live with their boyfriend abusers. Rather, unless they have married, they typically live with their families. The fact that a teenage woman lives at home and not with her boyfriend is legally significant because domestic violence laws, generally believed to be applicable to teens as well as adults, really only apply to partners sharing the same household.

Some states such as Illinois offer a broader interpretation of who can be protected from an abusive intimate partner. The *Illinois Domestic Violence Act of 1986*, for example, specifies that "family or household members" include "persons who have or have had a dating or engagement relationship."[4] Rather than excluding individuals who are in a violent dating relationship but who are not living together, this act broadens the definition of who can be involved in a domestic violence dispute by including young women. As defined, it also seems to offer some redress for people who are dating each other and not living together, even if they are teens.

SEEKING PARENTAL CONSENT

Even in states that have statutes that would seem to cover teenage women who find themselves in violent dating relationships, one of the first forms of redress remains closed to teens unless they have parental involvement. Specifically, only a limited number of states allow minors to apply for orders of protection in their own names. In most states, teenage women, as minors, cannot get an order of protection against an abuser unless they have the consent of a parent or guardian.

Obtaining parental consent can be problematic. In some cases, the attitudes of the teenage woman herself can stop her from seeking help from her parents. In other cases, the problem is related to the way parents react to their daughter's explanation of the causes of the situation.

Many teenage women, like adults involved in abusive situations, are confused about their respective boyfriend's treatment of them. Is their boyfriend's behavior a sign of love and concern or is it the unwelcome expressions of power and control? Was their boyfriend's rage an atypical episode when he just "went ballistic," or is there a pattern of abusive behavior? Even more than adults, many teens would prefer to hide such confusion from others. They may be embarrassed by what is happening to them. They may think they should be able to manage these types of private affairs themselves.

In contrast to adults, however, many teens are suspicious and mistrustful of adults in general, no matter how well intentioned the adults might seem. Moreover, unlike adults, many teens are worried that, even if they tell adults about their situations, the adults will ignore them, rebuff them for exaggerating their situations, accuse them of lying, or even ground them for being the victim of behaviors they did not cause.

Finally, as my research data clearly indicate, teenage women are worried that revealing abusive dating relationships to their parents could result in parental retaliation against their boyfriends. "I just know if I told my dad, he would kill him. Honestly, he'd go right over to his house and kill him or, if not, my boyfriend would be so badly injured that he would wish he were dead."

Sometimes a parent's behavior toward a daughter involved in a violent dating relationship seems to reflect a lack of concern or love for them. More often than not, however, parents are simply unaware of the extensiveness of teen dating violence and the fact that it can occur between young women and young men who come from ostensibly good homes. Moreover, parents can be manipulated, even as their daughter is manipulated, into believing that the boyfriend is charming because abusers can adopt an "Eddie Haskell" or "Dr. Jekyll and Mr. Hyde" persona. In adopting the persona of Eddie Haskell or Dr. Jekyll, the abuser exhibits a respectful, caring, and considerate demeanor to the family and friends of his partner but assumes a violent persona with his girlfriend. In fact, this thoughtful and caring "knight in shining armor" is probably the very persona that initially attracted the young woman. Over time, however, a victim of teen dating violence sees not only the respectful and caring side that her family members see but also the manipulative, controlling, and sometimes violent side that is the abusive "Mr. Hyde," or the real "Eddie Haskell," who is crude, self-focused, and abusive with his buddies.

BECOMING AN EMANCIPATED ADULT

A minor can act as an adult and on her own behalf if the courts emancipate her. Emancipation means that, in the eyes of the law, a minor becomes an adult and has all the rights and privileges of an adult. For example, the *Emancipation and Mature Minors Act in the State of Illinois* allows minors 16 years old and older to obtain the legal status of an adult if the minor "has demonstrated the ability to manage [her or] his affairs apart from a parent or guardian."[5] However, unless the minor has been automatically emancipated by marriage or by entry into the United States Military—actions that, in themselves, normally require parental consent—the minor still has to obtain the consent of her parents or guardian to apply for emancipation.

Thus, minors who, in theory, are allowed redress by the courts for intimate partner violence are, in practice, excluded from it without parental involvement. Further, the feelings attendant to any embarrassing self-revelation serve as a major impediment to any teenage woman trying to extricate herself from a violent dating relationship, whether by seeking advice from adults or by trying to get an order of protection against her abuser. Even in states where laws apparently protect those who do not technically fit the definition of domestic violence, such as teenage women living apart from their abusers, a minor's ability to seek legal redress is more theoretically than practically available.

FACING UNSYMPATHETIC AND CONFUSED COURTS

Should a young teenage woman find support from her parents or guardian, and should these adults agree to seek an order of protection or some other form of legal remedy against the abuser, a teenage plaintiff should not necessarily expect the courts to understand or to be sympathetic to her problem. Moreover, the courts are not always clear about the processes they need to follow when responding to a petition for an order of protection from a minor. Sousa (1999) describes specific situations that occur in a teen's life that courts seldom consider:

> Even if statutes were changed to give teens access to protective orders, the fact remains that prosecutors, defense attorneys, and judges often do not treat dating violence as a serious offense. If restraining orders are issued, they do not consider adolescent activities. For example, judges fail to ask the young victim what school classes she may have with the defendant, whether she wants the defendant to stay away from her at school, where the victim's school locker is in relation to the defendant's, what route or bus they take to school, what lunch period they have, or what extracurricular and after-school activities they share. This information would help the court design an order with far greater potential to be effective.[6]

Moreover, in violent teen dating relationships when minors are involved, it is often not clear whether a court will adjudicate the dispute at all. If it does, there usually remains a question about which court will hear the petition.

In the first instance, even when teens call the police, and when they have the support of an adult and can, at least theoretically, apply for legal redress, "the cases may not be charged or prosecuted."[7] Rather, the judge may either dismiss the case or suggest that the involved parties handle the case informally outside of court.

In the second instance, when the judge actually thinks that the courts should intervene formally, he or she must consider whether to refer the case to the civil, juvenile, or criminal courts. In cases where the petition is referred to a civil court, a complication with the plaintiff's relationship to the abuser again arises because not all states "authorize minors to seek civil orders of protection unless they are married, living with the abuser, or have a child in common with the abuser."[8] Further, in dating situations where a young woman applies for a civil restraining order, the process can be cumbersome and costly, and remedies available under civil protection orders may not be available.[9]

In reality, most teen dating violence cases come under the purview of the juvenile courts and are treated as "routine juvenile offense[s]."[10] These trials are apt to be more informal than adult criminal proceedings.

> The court and prosecutors may fail to establish the types of detention or conditions of release in juvenile cases which are more routinely imposed in adult criminal domestic violence cases. Juveniles are more likely to be released into the custody of their parents and specific conditions of release designed to protect the victim are not put into place. . . . In addition, those juveniles found guilty of committing offenses involving dating violence do not generally receive a disposition which effectively deals with the problem. Adolescents are frequently placed on probation or home supervision without regard to the potential for contact between the victim and the offender.[11]

Contrary to circumstances where both the offender and the victim are juveniles, an adult offender will always be prosecuted through the adult criminal system, even when the victim is a minor.[12]

Thus, a minor's access to a legal system, access that presumably protects her from a violent teen dating relationship, is limited in practice by statutory definition; by the attitudes of those affected by teen dating violence, whether the perpetrators are teens or adults; and by the question of jurisdiction. Each of these factors impedes a minor's ability to protect herself, especially if she seeks help from the courts.[13]

Accessing Social and Health Care Services

Minors involved in violent dating relationships have less access to health care and social services than do adults in similar situations. Nonprofit organizations funded by private donations and grants from the government and governmental organizations themselves have only recently become much more attentive to the needs of women and children trying to disengage from violent intimate partners. While these organizations have been very responsive to adult women and their children, they have not been as responsive to the needs of minors involved in violent dating relationships.

SOCIAL SERVICES

Domestic violence shelters or shelters for homeless people do not usually admit women under the age of 18 unless they are the children of adult women who are themselves fleeing abusive relationships. Even with parental permission, shelters are reluctant to house minors because the facilities do not meet the zoning, licensing, or building codes for housing children, or because it is too costly to construct facilities that meet the code requirements for housing teens.

In researching the availability of resources to help teenage women separate themselves from violent dating relationships, the Center for Impact Research found that there is a lack of permanent housing and other services that are specifically designed for teens.[14] Even fewer resources are available to unmarried, pregnant, or parenting teens who are not living with their parents or guardians. Those shelters that do house teens trying to escape abusive situations not only face more stringent building and zoning codes but also incur higher construction and staffing costs. Should a shelter take in an unemancipated minor or a minor without parental consent, the facility may be violating local and state laws.

Further complicating an institutional response to the plight of a teenage woman fleeing from a violent dating relationship is the fact that minors who are absent from their homes without the permission of their parents for protracted periods of time can be construed as runaways. If the minor is under the age of 16, then she may also be considered truant. Teens seeking social services, therefore, not only find such services few in number but also risk running afoul of the law if they need to leave their homes to access them.

HEALTH CARE SERVICES

Because of the emotional and psychological damage that intimate partner abuse inflicts on its victims, and even more because of the physical and sexual abuse that some young teenage women encounter while dating abusive partners, teens may often need to access mental and medical health care services. However, as the Center for Impact Research found, resources available to treat a teen's mental or physical health are limited. Further, the processes for accessing these services are especially confusing for both the teens and the health care workers who are committed to helping them.[15] Most of this confusion occurs among high school counselors, social workers, and psychologists, who are readily accessible at school, who want to help teens involved in violent dating relationships, and who are legally responsible mandated reporters.

ISSUES OF MANDATED REPORTING

"Human service professionals, including psychologists, social workers, counselors, teachers, nurses, and psychiatrists are required to report known or suspected child abuse in all 50 states."[16] These individuals are known as mandated reporters and, because of their positions of trust and their access to minors, are charged with the protection and safety of children.

However, does teen dating violence constitute child abuse and, therefore, require action by mandated reporters? If it does not, then do these adults nevertheless have a professional or ethical obligation to report suspected abuse? What are the "best practices" that mental health care practitioners, whether affiliated with schools or independent of them, should adopt to help a teenage woman separate herself from an abusive partner? The answer to each of these questions is contingent on the first: Does teen dating violence constitute child abuse?

At the national level, the *Child Abuse and Prevention and Treatment Act of 1974*, which "set the standard for state mandatory reporting laws,"[17] defined child abuse as follows:

> The physical or mental injury, sexual abuse, negligent treatment, or maltreatment of a child under the age of 18 by a person who is responsible for the child's welfare under circumstances which indicate the child's health or welfare is harmed or threatened thereby as determined in accordance with regulations prescribed. [18]

Does teen dating violence fit such a definition? The answer would seem to be "No." Teen dating violence does not constitute child abuse because, while the injury that is inflicted on the victim is not accidental, neither is it usually inflicted "by a parent or other person responsible for [the child's] care."[19] The law forbids dating a parent or guardian. Therefore, teen dating violence does not constitute child abuse. Furthermore, mandated reporters such as teachers, counselors, and social workers, are not required to inform state welfare authorities if they suspect incidents of teen dating violence.

PROFESSIONAL AND ETHICAL RESPONSIBILITIES

If teen dating violence does not constitute child abuse, and mandated reporters are legally absolved from the responsibility of reporting its occurrence to state child welfare authorities, then do these adults, especially those in contact with teens through high schools, have a professional or ethical responsibility to report suspected abusive dating relationships between teens? If so, under what specific circumstances? For example, does a mental health provider, counselor, social worker, or teacher have an obligation to notify a teen's parent or guardian of any form of dating violence, regardless of the type or frequency? Alternatively, do they only have this duty when the behavior suggests the likelihood of severe injury or death? What happens in cases where adults

have promised confidentiality, even though most counselors would not recommend making such a promise to a teen? Must they maintain confidentiality
under all circumstances?

According to several mental health care workers whom I interviewed,
counselors clearly believe they have a professional and ethical responsibility
to help teens in trouble, even if they are legally excused from making a response. However, at least initially, such a response does not usually include
notifying the parent of the teen's predicament. Rather, the consensus among
most mental health providers seems to be that high school mental health professionals should work with teens to get them to acknowledge and understand
their problems, and encourage them to talk willingly to their parents or guardian. With regard to confidentiality, most counselors would agree that they
would take the approach of telling teens, at the very start of the process, that
they cannot promise to keep everything confidential. This would be especially true if a teenage woman were to reveal something that indicated the
possibility of physical harm, whether to the teen herself or to another. Under
these circumstances, most counselors agree that they would have to "break
confidence" and inform the parents and, possibly, other authorities such as
the police.

However, if a counselor is disinclined to notify a parent, as many are,[20] then
the counselor still has other competing ethical and professional obligations,
even if not mandated by child abuse laws. Specifically, throughout the time
that a teenage woman meets with a high school counselor or social worker,
there may be a question about whether such visits constitute treatment or
therapy rendered by a mental health professional. If such conversations are
considered treatment or therapy—and it may be difficult to know when a
"conversation" ends and therapy or treatment begins—then a teen may be en-
titled to see a counselor for a specific number of times, usually six, without parental notification. After that, the counselor is legally required to notify the
teen's parents that their daughter is "in counseling" in order for the visits to
continue. While it is difficult to know when therapy begins, it is also not clear
whether the counselor needs to inform the parents that the subject of the therapy is teen dating violence.

In the course of talking to/treating a teen, a mental health care professional
such as a school counselor continuously tries to assess whether and to what extent the physical safety of her young client is in jeopardy. If conversations with
the teen suggest that there is the potential for a lethal outcome, and if the teen
cannot be persuaded to inform her parents of the problematic relationship,
then counselors generally agree that they should notify the teen's parents, even
if parental notification compromises the confidentiality promised to that teen.

Thus, it is conceivable that a teenage woman could talk about her involvement in a violent dating relationship and not reveal the violence or potential lethality of her situation to her parents. However, it is unlikely that her parents would remain uninformed because counselors would generally be willing to break confidentiality and inform parents of a serious situation that involves the health and safety of their daughter.

Once notified that the teen is involved in a violent, if not potentially lethal, dating relationship, the teen's parents can then make the decision about whether and in what manner they should respond. Assuming that the young teenage woman is suddenly forthcoming about her situation, a rather unlikely response from one who has just been "betrayed" by a trusted adult, then the teen's parents may act or refuse to act. If the teen's parents decide to act, then they may listen sympathetically and actively. They may be willing to talk with the offender or his family. They may even be willing to call the police. Without research, it is impossible to say which approach parents would be most likely to take and what the outcome would normally be. If the law enforcement community becomes involved, however, it is somewhat easier to envision either one of two scenarios: Either the law enforcement community deals informally with the report, as described earlier, or it deals formally with the complaint by reviewing a request for an order or protection. Given the lack of sympathy of the courts toward the problem of teen dating violence and its confusion about how and in what court to adjudicate the complaint, what happens at this point is anybody's guess.

If the teen's parents refuse to act and the teen continues to suffer physical or sexual abuse, then, at least in theory, it is possible that the teen's parents can be charged with the "failure to protect" a minor. By the time such legal steps have been taken, however, it is likely that the violence experienced by the young woman will have escalated to the point where the preemptive actions of the police or courts will be ineffective and, unfortunately, then the focus will shift from prevention and remediation to the punishment of the abuser.

Although young women theoretically have access to legal and social services to help them safely separate from violent dating partners, the reality is quite different. Because most teenage women involved in these relationships are minors, they must first obtain parental consent before they can access the legal and social service network that has been established to assist adult victims of domestic violence. Unfortunately, there are many reasons why teens prefer to keep their own counsel and are reluctant to involve their parents, their teachers, or their counselors in their problems. Even when teens try to act as adults by requesting emancipation, parental consent must be obtained before the courts can hear the petition. Thus, most of the remedies available to adult women suffering abuse in domestic violence situations are not readily available to teens involved in violent dating relationships. At first glance, a system appears to be in place that responds to all those involved in abusive dating relationships. However, a second and more informed look reveals that the existing system, while responsive to the needs of many adult women in these situations, is not responsive to the unique needs of teens in similar situations.

CHAPTER 4

TEEN DATING VIOLENCE RESEARCH: FINDINGS AND LIMITATIONS

"I am glad you are working on teen dating violence. It's a real problem. So many of our young women are involved in it, but it is difficult to convince them—or their parents—that it is a problem."

A high school counselor in a relatively affluent girls' Catholic high school greeted me with these words when I came to administer my survey on teen dating violence to some of her students. While introducing a teen dating violence prevention curriculum to the school, I was also interested to learn how pervasive teen dating violence was among high school students. Although research on the overall problem of domestic violence has increased over the past several years, there is a lack of information about the issues specific to teen dating violence. Distinct from domestic violence, what do we know about teen dating violence?

As Chapters Two and Three illustrate, teen dating violence and domestic violence share many similarities. Specifically, they share similarities in their causes, in their characteristics, and in their effects on the victims. Teen dating violence and domestic violence differ, however, in the effectiveness of policies and programs that have been designed to redress violence between intimate partners. Specifically, policies and programs designed to address the problem of domestic violence are, in most cases, ineffective vehicles for helping female minors under the age of 18 separate themselves from abusive dating relationships.

Besides the differences in accessing social programs and the legal system, teen dating violence and domestic violence differ in another respect. They vary in the quality and quantity of data researchers have collected about these problems. The types of information available to those who want to assist young teenagers in their struggles to extricate themselves from violent dating relationships are more limited. Thus, our ability to define the scope of the teen dating violence, to respond to it more precisely, and to address the problem as distinct from domestic violence, is currently limited. Further, because data about teen dating violence are often extrapolated from estimates of domestic violence, those who want to help teens do not yet have a refined concept of the incidence of dating violence and how teenage women experience it. Consequently, it has been more difficult to develop programs and policies to remediate or prevent teen dating violence.

In general, why have there been so relatively few data collection efforts on the problem of teen dating violence? Why have many of the studies been only marginally helpful? There are several reasons why it is difficult to quantify the scope of teen dating violence. One set of the reasons that I will discuss later in this chapter is related to the logistical, methodological, and ethical difficulties a researcher confronts when conducting research with minors. These difficulties either deter research efforts on the subject or, for the efforts that have been made, result in underestimates of its incidence. A second set of reasons that I address here concerns whether and how we conceptualize the problem of teen dating violence.

Conceptualizations of Teen Dating Violence

AN "ADULT" PROBLEM

Battering among intimate partners has typically been considered an "adult" problem. When one's concept of a problem defines it as being "adult," it is understandable that people who work directly with teens or who serve their interests indirectly as policy makers and lawmakers, have little incentive to gather data or to learn how teen dating violence differs from the adult version of the problem. In addition, the problem of teen dating violence is largely unrecognized and underresearched relative to domestic violence because many of us cannot imagine what it is like to be a teen in today's world, what it is like to be a teen engaged in a dating relationship, or how such a relationship might turn sour or violent.

NOT GRAPHICALLY NEWSWORTHY

One can hardly live in this country and be unaware of the numerous school shootings that now pepper even the quietest and most unassuming communities. Broadcasters and journalists lead with such violence because it evokes raw emotion and because it seems to affect large numbers of young people who arise, as they do each morning, to embark upon a typical day of school. Through no fault of their own, their days are anything but typical as they become victims of physical or emotional violence. By contrast, the problem of teen dating violence goes unrecognized, not only because it is assumed to be an adult problem, but also because it pales in graphic and horrific detail to these and other forms of violence that involve teens. As such, school shootings and gang-related violence that result in the death of innocent bystanders are perceived as random acts of violence. Instead of looking at these events and concluding that, despite the attention they receive in the media, the probability of becoming involved in such horrors is relatively low, we focus on the enormity of the loss and inflate the probability that such violence could happen to us or to our children. Subsequently, we become more threatened and fearful of being a victim of a school shooting or street violence, even when the data suggest that we are more likely to be murdered or harmed by someone we know well than by someone we may not know at all.

Thus, because of the way the media provide intense and extensive coverage to school shootings, we respond with a kind of fear that makes us believe that there is a greater probability of this type of violence occurring in our own communities. In fact, the probability of a teen's becoming a victim in a school shooting is far less than becoming a victim to teen dating violence. Nevertheless, the media are not as inclined to publicize the personal horror of teen dating violence. Rather, they do not deem the interpersonal violence that occurs between teens as newsworthy if it occurs one-on-one rather than in a group; if it occurs privately rather than in a social context where many teens can witness it; and if it develops over an extended period of time rather than in one terrible moment. Teen dating violence may "bleed," but it is an invisible hemorrhage as far as the media are concerned.

When the media do report an incident of teen dating violence, they usually do so in the context of a feature story about the connection between date rape and the use of drugs such as Ecstasy, or when a "rave" party results in a number of sexual assaults or injuries. Surely, the media provide a service when they publicize the perils of such activities. However, for those people whose views of the world are shaped largely by the media, such reporting can divert attention from other equally destructive individual acts of violence that often occur during the years of teen dating. In the absence of information sources that apprise parents, teachers, counselors, and policy makers of the prevalence of teen dating violence, we too easily ignore a problem that, researchers suggest, may affect between one and two-thirds of our high school teens.

A CULTURE OF SILENCE

Prevailing attitudes in the United States and the way in which we decriminalize crimes that occur within families or between intimate partners is a third
reason that helps to explain why so little research has been done on the problem of teen dating violence. Similar to domestic violence, teen dating violence
is often deemed by others as a personal matter between the partners, and one
that should be "kept in the family." Thus, even when family members of teens
involved in violent dating relationships do not dismiss abusive behaviors as
"puppy love," they may often be unwilling to consider behaviors such as stalking, beating, and sexual abuse as criminal. Such judgments do not, however,
excuse or decriminalize patently criminal behaviors. Nor do they relieve individuals from the moral, if not the legal obligation, of reporting what they see
to the police.

When outsiders who witness incidents of dating or domestic violence fail to
report them to the police, they reinforce the conspiracy of silence in our culture that seems to equate respect for another with disengagement or the unwillingness to become involved. Because few bother or consider it their place
to report the batteries and intimidation they see, relatively few incidents of
teen dating violence appear in crime reports. Thus, the magnitude of the
problem of teen dating violence is underestimated and the problem itself continues to be unrecognized as a social problem.

As an example of how teens and others may mistake disengagement and silence for respect and concern for others, I share a story reported to me by a
domestic violence counselor: Several teens were at a party at somebody's
house where the parents were not home. A young teen named "Laurie" and
her brother and sister were in attendance at the party. As the evening pro-
gressed, the party spilled over from the first floor to the second floor where
the family bedrooms were located. Laurie was upstairs and soon found herself
in a bedroom with several young men. The young men assaulted and took
turns raping Laurie. Throughout the ordeal, Laurie never called out to anyone for help, although she knew her brother and sister were downstairs.

Laurie reported the gang rape to the police. When an officer asked her why
she did not call for help, she told the officer, "I didn't want to embarrass the
boys." Laurie sacrificed her emotional and physical well-being to avoid embarrassing a group of young men who were guilty of criminal assault. Apparently, her notion of respect meant being silent while a horrible crime was
being committed. In order to "respect" the feelings of those who might be
embarrassed if they were caught in the act, Laurie maintained the code of silence and protected those who demonstrated their lack of respect for her by
engaging in criminal sexual assault.

Thus, there are three reasons related to our attitudes and culture that make teen dating violence difficult to quantify, even for those who recognize the problem: the perception that intimate partner abuse is an "adult" problem; the fact that such interpersonal violence is not generally deemed newsworthy; and the culture of silence that equates respect for others with the refusal to "embarrass" those whose behaviors are abusive. Regardless, however, the result is the same: Relatively little is known about the incidence of teen dating violence. Consequently, our abilities to help teens by designing and implementing appropriate public policies and programs are limited.

Teen Dating Violence: What We Have Learned So Far

Recognizing that we know relatively little about teen dating violence, especially in comparison to domestic violence, what can we ascertain from the information that we do have, whether interpolated from national databases or presented as conclusions from research using sample data? What, specifically, are the limitations of the research we have on teen dating violence, and what additional information would help us to design more effective programs and policies to address the problem?

In addition to stories and anecdotes shared among teens or discussed quietly in the faculty lounges of our high schools, there are three major sources of data and research that begin to profile the scope of teen dating violence. First, there are national databases. An example of such a national database is the National Crime Victimization Survey collected by the Department of Justice. Second, a plethora of statistics, both cited and not cited, is available to teens and adults alike on the Internet. The third source is scholarly research conducted on samples of teenagers. The survey data I collected for my research fall into this latter category.

NATIONAL DATABASE STATISTICAL FINDINGS

National crime statistics, including those that report the victimization of women, are typically compiled from crime data reported by local police departments. Local and state health departments may also collect data on the numbers and types of victimizations of women. Their sources generally include survey data that they collect, data phoned in on domestic violence hotlines, and data collected from local health care providers who treat women at emergency rooms or health care clinics. What can we learn from these different types of data collection efforts?

Young Women Are Frequent Victims. Of the many conclusions that researchers can draw from the data sources that document the victimization of women, the most disturbing one for those concerned about the well-being of teenagers is that the majority of victims of rape and other forms of sexual assault are young women, teens, and children. Data from a 1997 Department of Justice survey illustrate how vulnerable young women are to sexual victimization.[1] Specifically, the Department of Justice reported that 52 percent of all rapes and sexual assault victims were females under the age of 25. "Of the women who reported being raped at some point in their lives, 22 percent were under 12-years-old, and 32 percent were 12- to 17-years-old when they were first raped."[2] Over half (54%) of female rape victims were sexually assaulted before the age of 18.[3]

Analysis of national data that is more representative of teenagers reveals that 20 percent of the sexual assaults of young women under the age of 25 take place among young people between the ages of 12 and 17. Eighty percent (80%) occur among women between ages 18 and 24. Thus, at least one in every 89 females in the United States between ages 12 and 24 is a victim of a rape or other form of sexual assault. Another way of looking at these statistics indicates that there are 3.6 sexual assaults or rapes for every 1,000 women aged 12 to 14 and 5.9 sexual victimizations for every 1,000 females from the ages of 15 to 17. In a study using 1992–1993 data, Bachman and Saltzman (1995) reported that there were over 500,000 incidents where females age 12 and over experienced some form of sexual assault or rape. [4]

Victims Often Know Their Assailants. While it is still difficult to get good estimates of the incidence of teen dating violence, the existing data suggest that most women know their assailants. Specifically, according to a revised National Crime Victimization Survey, "29 percent of all victimizations against women were committed by a lone offender who was an intimate partner (husband, ex-husband, boyfriend, ex-boyfriend) of the victim."[5] Additionally, a 1994 study revealed that 24 percent of all violent rapes and sexual victimizations of a female were by an intimate,[6] a figure similar to the 26 percent reported in the 1992 study.[7] Further, "violence at the hands of an intimate involved about nine in 1,000 women annually. This translates into about 1 million women who are victims of such violence every year."[8]

Although these statistics help us to better understand the prevalence of violence against women by intimate partners, they do not help us understand the extent to which teens and minors are victimized by partners known to them. However, they do show that younger women are more likely to *report* their offenders than older women. Specifically, "women age 12 to 18 were more likely than women older than 18 to report violence against them by friends or acquaintances."[9] A study by Craven (1992), however, further suggests that many teen victims of intimate partner violence are also likely to know those who assault them. Specifically, Craven reports that "the intimate offender was more likely a boy/girlfriend or ex-boyfriend/girlfriend (14.3%) than a spouse (7.3%)."[10] Nevertheless, because of the general reluctance of a victim to disclose violence by her partner, a condition that is even more true of a spouse than of a dating partner, the number of women who know their abuser is probably underestimated.[11]

While many, but not most, young women are apt to report an intimate partner who is a sexual abuser, we nevertheless know very little about the teen dating violence that exists in forms other than sexual abuse. The exception to this is homicides between intimate partners. Here, researchers tell us that 28 percent of all females who were victims of homicide were murdered by husbands, ex-husbands, or boyfriends.[12] Within this category, however, there has been no determination of the percentage of such homicides that occur in teen dating relationships.

Female Victimizations Know Few Socioeconomic Distinctions. In addition to the fact that young women are more likely to be abused and to know their abusers than older women, the national data also suggest that intimate partner violence is found in all socioeconomic, racial, and ethnic groups. For the period 1992–1993, for example, "black and white women and Hispanic and non-Hispanic women sustained about the same amount of violence by intimate partners."[13] Not unexpectedly because of the strains and stresses that are associated with poverty, people who are economically impoverished tend to experience more intimate partner abuse than people in higher income brackets. Specifically, "women with annual family incomes under $10,000 were more likely to experience violence by an intimate partner than those with an income of [over] $10,000."[14] It is not clear, however, whether teens from lower income families also experience or report higher levels of violence than teens in higher income families. In Chapter Six, I explore the relationships between income and violence in dating relationships among teens.

Web Site Data

The Internet now abounds with Web sites where teens, parents, and counselors can obtain information about teen dating violence. But how good or accurate is this information? Are these sources any better at distinguishing between domestic violence and teen dating violence? Other than sexual victimization, do they have any measures of the manifestations of intimate partner abuse among teens? In accessing some of the data sources on the Web, it seems that most of the information is drawn either from national data sources and, consequently, has the limited usefulness of the data sources discussed above, or comes from Web sites that do not cite the sources of their information. A sample of such Web site statistical data follows:

- At least one in 10 teens will be involved in an abusive relationship.[15]
- 95 percent of the time, it's a boyfriend abusing a girlfriend.[16]
- Nonsexual courtship violence ranges from 9 percent to 65 percent, depending on whether definitions include verbal, emotional, or physical violence.[17]
- "A study of 8th and 9th grade male and female students indicated that 25 percent had been victims of nonsexual dating violence and 8 percent had been victims of sexual dating violence."[18]
- "The average prevalence rate for nonsexual dating violence is 22 percent among male and female high school students."[19]

While such information may be accurate, it is difficult to assess its credibility when Web site authors do not cite their sources.

Findings from Research with Sample Data

Even as domestic violence research is increasing, academic researchers are giving increased attention to measuring the incidence of teen dating violence by using samples of teenagers. These estimates and the extent to which it is possible to generalize from the data, however, vary widely depending on the nature of the sample, how the research was conducted, and how the constructs of "teen," "dating," and "violence" are defined and utilized. Nevertheless, such research provides a baseline for making estimates about the incidence of teen dating violence. What, then, does such research suggest?

Using a broad definition of teenage women as being those females who have not yet reached the legal age of majority or 18 years of age, and including all forms of dating violence—emotional/psychological, physical, and sexual violence—Kuehl (1991) suggests that at least one in three females under the age of 20 will experience some kind of violence at the hands of her boyfriend before she reaches adulthood.[20] Another study of both males and females and using a measure of dating violence that included physical and sexual forms of violence estimated that from one-third to almost 60 percent of teens experienced dating violence. Levy (1991) estimated that as many as one-third of all high school students experienced some form of physical or sexual violence in their teen dating relationships.[21] Somewhat higher estimates were reported by Jezl, Molidor, and Wright (1996). They found that slightly over 59 percent of their sample of male and female high school students experienced some form of dating violence within the past year.[22]

When examining the incidence of physical abuse only, Molidor and Tolman (1998) estimate that the percentages of high school students experiencing physical abuse were 36.4 percent for girls and 37.1 percent for boys.[23] Suderman and Jaffe (n.d.) found that 21 percent of all girls had experienced some form of physical violence while dating in high school.[24] Significantly lower estimates were reported by Bergman (1992). Specifically, Bergman found that 15.7 percent of girls and 7.8 percent of boys experienced some physical violence while dating.[25] Had emotional/psychological abuse and sexual abuse been included in their constructs of teen dating violence, then the incidence of such violence would probably have been even higher for all reports.

In summary, researchers use a variety of measures and different samples to try to quantify the extent to which young people are involved in abusive or violent dating relationships. Unfortunately, the goals and samples of researchers sometimes differ, thus making it difficult to compare findings or to generalize to wider populations of teens. Regardless of how the data are measured and who constitutes the sample, however, the research consensus is that the problem is pervasive and that teen relationships can become very brutal.

Limitations of Existing Research

In addition to the different approaches that researchers take toward the task of measuring teen dating violence, there are other limitations to analyzing data from national sources and from research conducted directly with samples of teens. What are these limitations? Moreover, what are some of the logistical, methodological, and ethical problems researchers need to overcome in order to conduct research on teen dating violence, especially when using minors in their samples?

LIMITATIONS OF NATIONAL DATA COLLECTION EFFORTS

In general, there seem to be four limitations researchers encounter when analyzing data from national databases or when comparing the results from different research samples. I summarize and discuss each of them below.

First, many commonly used crime statistic sources do not provide the details of the context in which a crime was committed. Thus, it becomes difficult for researchers to distinguish a crime between intimate partners from a random crime involving victims and perpetrators who are strangers to each other.

Second, the way crime victims are categorized by age and by type makes it difficult to differentiate adult domestic violence from teen dating violence.

Further, some research focuses only on sexual victimizations to the exclusion of other forms of intimate partner violence such as emotional/psychological abuse and physical abuse.

Third, for teens as well as for adults, there are many reasons to keep silent about abusive relationships. Consequently, almost all researchers agree that estimates of teen dating violence are probably low and that no one knows the real numbers.

Fourth, health reports from city, county, and state medical facilities and agencies, while presenting different sources of information about physical and sexual violence, are also far from perfect measures of intimate partner violence. Not only do few health care providers know how to look for the signs of intimate partner abuse when women appear at emergency rooms, but also hospital record-keeping processes vary in quality and type from one facility to another.

Context of Victimization Is Often Undefined. One reason that the incidence of teen dating violence may be unreported or underreported is that the context in which the victimization occurs is not always described when crime statistics are reported by police departments or other law enforcement agencies, even when victimizations occur among adults. When such details are omitted, the context and, to some degree the causes of aggravated battery, sexual assault, or murder cannot be determined from most national statistics. Neither can such crimes be linked to intimate partner violence. Without context and some sense of causality, it thus becomes more difficult to design appropriate strategies to prevent intimate partner violence.

Only recently, and usually at the behest of women's rights organizations, have crime reporting agencies begun to report crime data that note when the violence occurs between intimate partners. For example, the National Crime Victimization Survey asks "more explicit and direct questions about sexual assaults and other victimizations perpetrated by known offenders."[26] In such cases, a victim's response to such questions makes it possible for researchers to identify whether there was a domestic or dating relationship between the perpetrator and the victim. Thus, better data are now available to estimate the incidence of domestic violence, although there is still a problem with estimating intimate partner violence among teenagers.

Age Categories Are Too Inclusive and Violence Categories Are Too Exclusive. Although better data are being collected to help identify the scope and characteristics of domestic violence, the way data are collected still does not allow us to make accurate distinctions between adults, teenage minors, and children involved in intimate partner violence. For example, national crime databases do not usually distinguish neatly between violence that affects children (those under the age of 13), minors (those under the age of 18), or teenagers (those above the age of 12 but under the age of 20). FBI Uniform Crime Reports use age categories where age 16 is a major breaking point, thus making it impossible to distinguish between teens who are minors and those who are not. Moreover, teens who are younger than 16 cannot be distinguished from children, some of whom may be involved in abusive relationships. When using such data, researchers must interpret the statistics as best they can to determine whether intimate partner violence occurred when the victim was a minor or an adult.

In addition to using age categories that do not distinguish between adults and minors, national crime victimization data focus more on sexual victimizations than on other forms of intimate partner violence. These other forms of domestic violence include physical abuse, battery, assault, and murder, and are often estimated from other data sources rather than from direct reports. Furthermore, while admittedly difficult to measure, emotional and psychological abuse are nevertheless forms of intimate partner violence that do not typically appear in crime reports at either the local or national levels.

Reluctance to Report Victimizations. A third reason that complicates researchers' abilities to provide accurate estimates of teen dating violence is that many women, including teens, do not report their victimizations to the police or to health care personnel, even when they need medical care. In general, women are discouraged from reporting their victimizations to law enforcement authorities because of "the private nature of the event, the perceived stigma associated with one's victimization, and the belief that no purpose will be served in reporting it."[27]

Adult abused women are embarrassed. They are frightened. They fear reprisals. In addition, as Alissa described in Chapter One, they often feel "crazy," hopeless, and believe that no one—including family members—will help them. Even the act of contacting a friend, let alone the police, becomes intimidating for women involved in abusive relationships. How much more intense must these feelings be for female teens in abusive relationships? The answer, undoubtedly, is that the teens are probably even more intimidated about speaking out than their adult counterparts.

Feelings of social opprobrium, embarrassment, and inefficacy are even stronger for teens than for most adults because teens are typically so concerned about avoiding appearances that will make them stand out from their peers. Because they do not want to distinguish themselves from their peers by reporting trouble in their dating relationships, even when these relationships become violent, they are likely to withdraw from the very people who are most able to support and counsel them. Moreover, because teens' world experiences are more limited than adults,' they are bereft of a good context against which to evaluate the appropriateness of their partners' behaviors. Consequently, what they themselves experience becomes "normal."

However, even when they believe that what they are experiencing is normal, a perception that would presumably make them more inclined to share their stories with others, they nevertheless isolate themselves from fellow teens. Without the social context that provides information that tells them they are not alone, teens are apt to become even more isolated than adult women involved in violent and controlling relationships. Thus, developmental factors, coupled with the fact that teens have limited recourse to the legal system without the permission of their parents, make it highly unlikely that teens will report victimization to their parents. Therefore, when teens or their parents do not report dating violence to the authorities, crime statistics about intimate partner violence are destined to be underestimated.

Even when a teen reports being victimized and her complaint is referred to the police, law enforcement officers themselves are often confused about the appropriate way to respond. When and how should they intervene? Should they first talk to the victim? To her parents? Or to the alleged perpetrator and his family? Such confusion about how to respond to teens, as discussed in Chapter Two, often results in the failure of law enforcement officials to report the incidence of dating violence for inclusion in crime statistics. This is yet another reason why the estimates of the incidence of dating violence are likely to be incorrect.

Limited Responsiveness from Health Care Providers. A fourth reason why teen dating violence is likely to be underreported is that even when researchers rely on data sources other than national crime statistics such as health statistics, these sources themselves can be highly inaccurate. For example, when violence occurs between adults, and victims seek medical care, hospital personnel sometimes do not look for or cannot tell whether a woman's injuries occurred because of intimate partner violence or for some other reasons. Moreover, even in cases where hospital workers strongly suspect abuse and try to raise the subject with the victim, adult women are extremely reluctant to tell health care workers that it was a partner who hurt them.

The major reason for withholding information about injuries that result from intimate partner violence is obvious: Women fear additional reprisals from the abuser once they have been discharged from the medical facility. As many emergency room workers who are attuned to the problem of intimate partner violence explain, one of the primary signs that a woman has been beaten by her partner and did not suffer a "fall" or other form of "accident" is her partner's unwillingness to leave the victim alone in the emergency room.

To the uninitiated, such an action could bespeak love and concern. Those who understand intimate partner violence, however, recognize that an abuser will not leave the side of the victim because the abuser does not want to give the woman a private moment when she might report the abuse to medical or law enforcement personnel.

Because teens are not likely to be accompanied to an emergency room by their abusers, they do not face the same type of intimidation as many adult women. Nevertheless, they are also fearful of reporting abuse as the cause of their injuries. Like adult female victims of domestic violence, young teens are embarrassed, afraid of reprisal, resist being lectured, or fear that they will be punished by their parents for causing harm to themselves when, in fact, they were not responsible for the violent attacks at the hands of their abusers. Thus, teens are also unlikely to report becoming a victim to their dating partners.

The problem of obtaining accurate data about intimate partner violence from medical providers is not only a function of the reluctance of the victims to report the crime or even of medical care workers to recognize it. It is also a function of the way medical records are kept in hospitals. Even when women or teens do report abuse, "the information may not be recorded in the medical record. Currently, standard systems are not in place to systematically record and count incidents of intimate partner violence in health care settings."[28]

For these reasons, health care statistics are as likely to underestimate the incidence of intimate partner violence in general, and among teens in particular, as are crime statistics. However, when interviewed about their experiences in emergency rooms and clinics, health care workers can be an important source of information about how intimate partner abuse occurs and of the details that comprise the context of intimate partner violence.

In summary, although helpful in distinguishing intimate partner abuse from random acts of violence perpetrated on women, national databases are limited in usefulness when researchers try to measure the incidence of dating violence among teens. The demand for better data would grow, however, if talk show hosts and women's organizations would make more attempts to draw attention to and lobby law enforcement agencies about the need to collect better data. By collecting data that differentiate teen dating violence from domestic violence, policy analysts would provide policy makers with better information that should result in better policy decisions.

Logistical, Methodological, and Ethical Research Problems

Virtually any researcher confronts logistical, methodological, and ethical problems when conducting research with human subjects. These problems are intensified, however, when the research involves human subjects who are minors, or when the topic of the research is sexual behavior.

LOGISTICAL PROBLEMS

When conducting any research with human subjects, researchers who are affiliated with universities or research institutions usually need to obtain the approval of an Institutional Review Board (IRB) or a Human Subjects Committee before they can proceed. At one time, IRBs were most active when the research proposal before them was medical or scientific in nature. This type of research usually involved drug or experimental medical treatments that were difficult for lay people to understand, probably physically invasive, perhaps painful, and maybe even potentially harmful to the subject.

With the exception of psychological research conducted on human subjects, however, the scrutiny IRBs gave to social scientific or policy research was relatively casual. In many cases, social science researchers never even went to IRBs for authorization before undertaking their research, especially survey research.

With the advent of increased scrutiny by the federal government, which funds many scientific and social scientific research studies, and the increased propensity for people to sue when they believe they have been harmed through someone's negligence, IRBs have become much more active in reviewing and authorizing social science research. Thus, it has become increasingly difficult for researchers, especially policy researchers, to ignore or to circumvent the role of IRBs.

The exercise of an IRB's authority is especially problematic for policy researchers, who often must produce policy research or analyses under daunting time constraints to influence decisions on pending legislation. Further, policy researchers can grow to resent the role of an IRB, which can be helpful but can also be officious or prone to acting beyond the scope of its charge or members' professional expertise. This is especially true when it is obvious that the research is not harmful, invasive, or covered by federal regulations for the protection of human subjects. Consider, for example, the "invasiveness" or potential harm to a subject when asking her or him to indicate anonymously political preferences, or to describe a preference for one brand of cellular phone over another. Another example is the possible irritation—and sometimes the delay—that is caused when a member of an IRB, instead of focusing on insuring that the rights of the human subjects have not been violated, insists on gender neutral language, even when the subjects of the survey all have the same gender. Nevertheless, whether fearful of lawsuits, overly conscientious, or overreaching in their critiques, IRBs often create unnecessary logistical obstacles, even for policy researchers who want to do the right thing in order to conduct ethical policy research.

With regard to the teen dating violence research that has been conducted, the concerns of the IRBs have been especially difficult to negotiate for two reasons: First, the subject of the study is sexual behavior; second, the human subjects in the research sample are minors.

When the subject of the research is sexual behavior, IRBs will probably react more skeptically and critically to the content of such protocols and surveys, "because of the perceived sensitive nature of sexuality surveys."[29] Such a reaction is characteristic despite the fact that "anonymous paper and pencil surveys are exempt from the federal regulations regarding the protection of human subjects."[30] Nevertheless, "they [IRBs] very often do not seem to treat such studies as truly exempt, and a written consent form is frequently required of researchers."[31] The effect is that research that needs to be conducted under strict time constraints is often delayed.

In the conduct of my research in teen dating violence, the university's IRB required me to draft a written consent form for the parents, although interestingly, not for the students or for the school. This consent form underwent several reviews and, because the university IRB met only monthly, resulted in significant time delays.

What, in particular, did the university IRB demand of me, even though paper and pencil surveys are exempt from federal guidelines? First, they wanted to review the survey instrument itself. Such a review was not unexpected. However, one member of the IRB objected to my operationalization of the concepts of violence because, he argued, I was making value judgments about behaviors such as sexual assault and judging them violent. His objection was that sexual assault or other behaviors might not be construed as violence depending on the cultural context in which the behavior occurred. Despite my argument that I was only asking teens to respond to their reactions to such "violence," I nevertheless had to reword several of the questions in my questionnaire in order to receive IRB approval because of objections that were more about methodological and disciplinary issues than ethical issues protecting human subjects.

A second objection arose when I explained my intention to ask questions of the teens, not only about their dating behaviors but also about how they saw their parents relating to each other. The reason for asking this set of questions was to study whether teens who saw domestic violence at home would be more or less inclined to accept abusive behaviors at the hands of their boyfriends. The IRB would not allow me to ask such questions unless I made the parents very aware of my intention to ask their children about their perceptions of their parents' interactions. Would I also need consent from the parents themselves in order to ask their children about how they see their parents interacting at home?

While often in disagreement about how to conduct survey research about sexual behavior, or about the extent to which I had to inform parents of the content in the survey their teens were taking, the IRB and I agreed in our concerns about how surveys should be administered to minors. I reserve most of the ethical concerns we raised in our discussions to a later section. In terms of logistical problems, however, let me here identify a few that are not typically part of conducting research with adult human subjects. These problems include locating parents and guardians to sign consent forms; getting the signed consent forms returned in a timely manner; checking parental signatures for authenticity; making provisions with the schools to supervise teens whose parents do not want them to be involved in the study; and minimizing peer pressure for students to participate in the study when they might prefer not to participate.

As with any research, there are a number of logistical problems involved in administering a survey that have nothing to do with methodological design. When conducting research using minors as human subjects, however, and when the subject of the research is as sensitive a subject as sexual behavior, these logistical problems become even more substantial. My research on teen dating violence, conducted with 499 female teenage minors, was no exception.

METHODOLOGICAL ISSUES

Because the logistics of sampling minors are more complicated than when surveying adults, it is not surprising that most researchers will look to elementary and secondary schools as a source of sample subjects. As samples of "convenience," these samples are not usually randomized and, as such, few statistical generalizations to larger populations can be drawn beyond the samples themselves. Consider, for example, the bias that is probably injected into a research design that does not include teens who are not currently attending high school. Perhaps the very reason that some of these teens have dropped out is to avoid contact with an abuser. Omitting data from these teens would surely bias survey results. Thus, to make sweeping generalizations about "all teens" would be methodologically misleading and irresponsible. Moreover, when the subject of the research is highly personal, as it is in teen dating violence, a number of respondents may deem the questions intrusive and refuse to answer some of them. Such selectivity in answering questions can result in biased results because it is often difficult to tell why respondents refused to answer and whether there was a pattern in the refusals.

When any survey researcher asks personal questions, for example, about one's age or income, some respondents may be less willing to respond than when they are asked less personal questions, for example, about their preferences for automobiles, political candidates, or cellular phone service. Refusals to answer questions about sexual behavior or participation in activities that could be deemed illegal, for example, one's use of drugs, are even more likely. When there are several nonresponses to a particular survey question, the results of the study may be biased.

Researchers have a number of methods for handling this methodological problem. While a critique of these methods is not germane to this general discussion of teen dating violence, it is nevertheless important to ask whether such a bias is likely to exist and, if it does, in what direction.

Despite the promise of confidentiality in my research, a few students made remarks to me or to others that suggested they were skeptical that the researchers would maintain confidentiality. Other students may have trusted that we would keep their confidence but may have been embarrassed to reveal their experiences. Such skepticism or potential for embarrassment suggests that some teens may not have responded to some of the questions or, if they did, gave false answers to cover their embarrassment.

Particular to the survey data I collected, a review indicates that, at most, less than one percent of the respondents failed to answer a particular question. Thus, nonresponse does not appear to be a major factor that could inject bias into the results. However, what about the respondents who, for any number of reasons, could have given false answers?

Although it is virtually impossible to estimate the number of teens who purposefully gave answers that did not reflect their true experiences or opinions, the best a researcher can hope for is that erroneous responses are random and, therefore, that they will cancel each other out. Thus, no bias would be introduced into the results from those included in the sample. However, there is still the problem of bias from those excluded from the sample because they do not currently attend high school. Moreover, because "girls do not reveal the victimization they experience"[32] to parents, to police, to teachers, or to health care workers, they may also be reluctant to reveal experiences of victimization to a researcher, even when promised confidentiality. Thus, if bias is present in my research, it is likely to be in the direction of underestimating the incidence of teen dating violence rather than overestimating it.

Samples of convenience, while limited in representativeness, are nevertheless useful in approximating the scope of teen dating violence. Because of the additional methodological complexities of conducting research with minors, however, researchers cannot be faulted too much for using such samples. More important than criticizing researchers for dealing with the limitations of data, however, is to recognize that the data they collect are more likely to underestimate the problem than to overstate it.

ETHICAL OBSTACLES

In conducting research with any human subject, and even more so with a minor, there are several ethical considerations that a researcher must anticipate. Three of the most prominent include obtaining the informed consent of the participants; insuring that the participants suffer no harm throughout the course of the research; and maintaining confidentiality.

Informed Consent. After researchers have created research designs, constructed a questionnaire, and identified a sample to survey, they often need to obtain the informed consent from survey participants. In general, to be "informed," research subjects should be told the general purpose of the research. Moreover, they should be told about the potential risks and benefits they might experience as a result of their participation.

Once informed, the consent requested of the subject may be either active or passive. Active consent means that the research subject needs to sign a statement in which, after having read it, he or she explicitly agrees to participate in the research. Passive consent, by contrast, means that the researcher can simply assume that the research subject is willing to participate in the protocol unless he or she signs a form to the contrary. Obviously, active consent is a far more stringent requirement for the conduct of research and, in the case of my research with teenage minors, was the type of consent required by my university's IRB.

Why did we insist on a consent form at all when federal guidelines do not mandate it for paper and pencil surveys? What was the IRB looking for in the consent form? Whose consent was required? The parents/guardians? The teens? Or both?

In general, the goal of the IRB was to insure that the research subjects were not exploited or harmed during the course of the research. To insure this, the members of the IRB wanted to make sure that my research protocol comported with the information I included in the consent form. For example, was it made clear to the parents/guardians that the teens would be taking a survey in class during school time? Was it clear that the school had authorized the administration of the survey? Was it clear that the contents of the survey would be about the teens' experiences while dating and not their perceptions of domestic interactions between their parents or other adults in their homes? Did the consent form clearly state the possible risks and benefits to the teen and to society of participating in the survey? Was the wording of the consent form sufficiently simple and devoid of research jargon so that an "average" person could understand what was being asked and what the potential benefits and risks were? Was it clear that a teen would incur no penalty or reprisal for failure to participate in the research? Was it clear that the teen could withdraw from the research at any time, again without penalty? Was what the teen would be doing during the research made clear? For example, would the subject see a film? Read materials? Ingest something? Or be subjected to stimuli?

From an ethical perspective, the IRB and I agreed that the best approach was to require the active consent of the teens' parents or guardians, even though the teens would be the ones taking the survey. Why did we require the consent of the parents/guardian and not simply the teens themselves? Moreover, why did we require *active consent*?

There were three reasons for our decision to require *parental/guardian consent*. First, teens may not foresee or be able to understand all the personal consequences of their participation in research. Second, even when consent forms are written in accessible and clear language that IRBs have reviewed many times, and even if the teens took the time to read them, many still may not be able to understand the content of the consent form. Third, because parents and guardians are ultimately responsible for the well-being and safety of minors, they should be fully informed about their child's participation in any activity that might even remotely affect her health and well-being.

We required *active* consent because we wanted to make sure that the adults responsible for the teens actually had the opportunity to see the consent form and communicate their decision regarding participation to us in writing. Because of our concern for the teens, we did not want to assume that the consent form reached the teen's home or, if it did, that it was seen by an adult. We did not want to assume that a parent or guardian consented to the research because there were too many reasons why a consent form might not have been returned to the school or to the researchers.

Although the IRB only required active informed consent from parents/guardians, I also sought consent from the teens themselves. Specifically, before the administration of the survey, I told teens that, regardless of whether their parents consented, each of them could subsequently make a decision about whether to participate. Of course, teens who wanted to participate when their parents/guardians objected were not allowed to participate.

Although no student refused an opportunity to take the survey after adult consent had been obtained, my interaction with the IRB did raise two important theoretical questions for me. First, in the conduct of our research with human subjects who are minors, can we "force" minors to participate when they do not want to, simply because their parents or guardians give consent for them to do so? Second, without obtaining the explicit permission of the minors themselves, are we unconsciously supporting the idea that adults can force them to participate when they may not want to do so?

The principle guiding my answer to these two questions is an ethical one: Always try to choose the option that enhances the dignity of the people with whom you are dealing. Thus, my answer to these questions is that research with human subjects should always err on the side of respecting the subjects. Although parents and guardians can speak for minors by consenting to their participation, a researcher should also respect the subject's wishes whenever he or she can express them. In the case of my research, I thought it respectful to ask the teens whether they wanted to participate. A second principle is also maintained: Because no research with human subjects should ever be coercive, teens should not be forced into participating in research, even when parents give consent. Neither should it be assumed that parental consent would signal the teen's consent.

In addition to such an approach, there are also clear legal reasons to have parents/guardians and teen participants be as fully informed as possible. Specifically, the litigious nature of our society dictates that the prudent researcher—and the prudent school principal—will do everything possible to inform those who have legal responsibility for a child about any "extraordinary" events that may arise during a normal school day. IRBs can be helpful to researchers in this regard because their participation indicates another level of review that makes accusation of negligence or child endangerment less credible.

Despite the best efforts of researchers, IRBs, and school principals to work together to conduct ethical and respectful research using minors as human subjects, none of these agents can control whether the parents/guardians actually read or understand the consent form. In some cases, there may be a lack of parental interest. Another reason, however, involves the construction of the consent form itself. In the case of my research, by the time I had finished an acceptable version, the consent form was over two single spaced pages in length. More than one teacher or administrator expressed concern about the length of the consent form. Even though written in "accessible" language, the length of the survey could, they warned, intimidate many parents. They could simply sign it without reading it. "Couldn't the form be shorter so that the parents would read and take the time to understand it?" they asked. "Yes," is my answer, but a shorter form would not have met all the requirements and concerns of the IRB. Ironically, in some cases, the IRB may have actually discouraged what it was trying to promote.

Of the over 500 forms sent out to parents, five did not give permission. Obviously, the rest either read the consent form and made an informed judgment, or they just signed it without reading it because it was simply too dense and time-consuming.

Maintaining Confidentiality. As any professional researcher knows, maintaining a promise of confidentiality in research is a key requirement for getting truthful responses and sensitive information, especially when the subject matter of the research is something exceedingly personal, embarrassing, or potentially indicting. If professionals such as lawyers, journalists, clergy, or therapists do not take promises of confidentiality seriously, they diminish the opportunities to search for truth, to redress grievances, and to promote justice and well-being. This is particularly true when those who make personal revelations risk their safety in doing so.

Despite the seriousness with which professionals rightly construe the promise to maintain confidentiality, the right to confidentiality is not absolute or without consequences. For example, at some point during therapy, clinical psychologists will usually tell a client that the right to confidentiality is not absolute and that there is a professional and ethical obligation to inform the appropriate parties if a client makes a credible threat to the life of another, or even threatens taking his or her own life. Journalists can be jailed when they refuse to reveal a source when there is a compelling state interest or a matter of national interest. But what are the professional and ethical obligations of social science researchers, including those who engage in survey research? Are social scientific researchers included among those professionals who operate in a privileged professional capacity? If so, under what conditions must they break confidentiality? Are there any professional or ethical standards that will help a researcher decide whether to maintain a promise of confidentiality to a minor? Under what circumstances must the researcher reveal what she or he has learned in the course of research?

These were troubling questions for me and for the IRB. For example, we anticipated the cases of teens who did not put their names on their surveys but whose responses nevertheless suggested that they might be involved in a questionable or even a violent dating relationship. Subsequently, we discussed whether I, as a social science researcher but as one untrained in the professions of counseling or psychology, had any obligation to review individual surveys and then make judgments about whether and to what degree a teen might be involved in some form of abuse. If there were a specific revelation, or even a suggestion of an abusive situation, was I obligated to do the detective work that would help identify the student or, at least, to narrow the list of suspects when there was no name or other identifying marks on the survey the teen returned? Having narrowed the "suspects" to a list of names or even to an individual, was I then obligated to notify anyone of my concerns? Whom should I notify? In general, were there any circumstances that would abrogate a survey researcher's promise of confidentiality to a minor when that minor, intentionally or unintentionally, reveals involvement in a potentially harmful situation?

While I know of no obvious answers to these questions, I believe that researchers should first follow the approach that clinical psychologists and counselors take with clients in therapy. Specifically, researchers should avoid making sweeping claims of confidentiality on consent forms when conducting research with minors as human subjects. Rather, we should inform them that we would hold their answers in confidence, except in cases where their responses indicate anything that could be construed as a physically violent or potentially lethal situation.

In cases where such qualifications have not been included on the consent form and the researcher obtains evidence that suggests a potentially lethal situation, I believe that a researcher is obligated to choose a child's well-being over any professional confidentiality guideline. Thus, if a minor reveals a potentially lethal situation, then the researcher should make efforts to identify the teen and talk with her about getting some help to extricate her from the situation. Should the teen be unwilling to cooperate, then the researcher should be required to notify the parents.

In my own research, a few teens stated that they had been or were currently involved in a violent dating relationship. In none of these cases, however, did we have reason to suspect a potentially lethal involvement. Perhaps then, my concerns and those of the university IRB were overstated. Nevertheless, obtaining the approval of the IRB required fairly time-consuming negotiations over a consent form that accurately represented how the researchers would use the data obtained in the research and, at the same time, protected the safety and well-being of the minors who served as human subjects.

Preparing for Emotional Harm. Because surveys on teen dating violence often ask teens to evaluate the appropriateness of behaviors that are emotionally, physically, or sexually abusive, researchers must anticipate ethical questions not only about informed consent and confidentiality but also about whether their research may inflict any harm on teens. For example, might a teen taking a survey realize, in the course of taking the survey, that she has been or is currently involved in an abusive situation? What is the likelihood that such a realization, rather than prompting a decision to seek help, would actually generate psychological harm or trauma to the respondent, either during or after the administration of the survey?

Unfortunately, there is little empirical evidence upon which to make such an estimate. Nevertheless, because minors are involved as human research subjects and because the subject of the research involves sexual behavior, IRBs will often frame the issue as if the risks of inflicting emotional damage on the respondent are great. For example, relative to medical research that is often physically invasive and poses the threat of physical harm, questionnaire studies, "(even those involving sexuality topics) are viewed as relatively benign."[33] However, when compared to the "relatively innocuous questions in marketing research, questions about sexual behavior can be viewed as riskier."[34] What survey research is considered so risky that it becomes legally imprudent or ethically objectionable to conduct?

According to federal guidelines, human subjects should be exposed to no more than "minimal risk" when participating in research. Here, minimal risk is "minimal" when "the probability and magnitude of harm or discomfort anticipated in the research are not greater in and of themselves than those ordinarily encountered in daily life or during the performance of routine physical or psychological examinations or tests."[35]

Apart from the physical expenditures of energy and, possibly eye strain and fatigue, does asking questions of minors about their dating behaviors expose them to minimal risk, or to some great risk of emotional discomfort or psychological harm?[36] As Weiderman (1999) notes, without objective criteria or data, "determining whether sexuality research constitutes more than minimal risk is a judgment call."[37] However, in a litigious society where anyone injured looks for recourse through the legal system, this is probably not a risk most IRBs, schools, or researchers are willing to take.

Therefore, in the survey research that I conducted, I tried to minimize the risk of psychological trauma or emotional discomfort for the teens participating in the research. Specifically, I arranged for a counselor to be present in the classroom during the administration of the survey. Further, I encouraged the teens to seek help from the counselor if anything troubled them after the administration of the survey.

After each class completed the survey, the teens were invited to ask questions about the research itself or about specific survey questions. One teen raised a question about the appropriateness of specific dating behaviors such as stalking. Another said she was concerned about a "friend who fit a lot of the stuff on the survey." Still another wanted to know why I had not asked questions about the dating violence girls inflict on boys. Sometimes the teens expressed annoyance, anger, or confusion about what they read on the survey. However, the questions most often raised were about why I asked questions about racial or ethnic identity.

When such questions arose in a group context, either the counselor or I answered their questions or encouraged them to think through their concerns and feelings in order to make their own judgments. When the teens seemed to have more questions than we could answer in a group context, or where a teen seemed to be troubled by our exchange with her, we suggested that she see either her teacher or the counselor. To be of assistance in such situations and prior to the administration of the survey, both of these types of educators had previously undergone a daylong workshop on teen dating violence.

As the data in Chapter Five will indicate, it was not surprising that only a few students accepted the invitation to talk further with their teachers or counselors about any matter related to the survey or to their personal situations. For those who did avail themselves of the opportunity, however, counselor follow-up was immediate and, apparently, helpful. For example, one counselor reported that of the teens who took the survey and, subsequently, were involved in a dating violence prevention program, two had now recognized the abusiveness of the relationships they were in and had begun intensive counseling. Another teen approached a counselor to work through a way of telling her parents that she was pregnant. Still another teen visited a counselor because she was worried about her mother who was involved in a violent relationship. In one instance, when a teen expressed a concern in the course of a class discussion that suggested that she might have a problem she needed to discuss with an adult, the counselor took the initiative to seek out the student.

None of these encounters with counselors occurred immediately after the administration of the survey. This fact suggests that no student experienced immediate or obvious harm while completing the survey. Similarly, none of the teens evinced obvious signs of emotional distress while they were taking the survey or after they had completed it.

Minimizing Peer Pressure. Although we asked the teens whether they wanted to take the survey, the act of raising hands and leaving the room to signal a decision not to participate might have been difficult in view of the peer pressure that could be exerted by classmates. To minimize the potential effects of peer pressure so that students could act freely and without coercion, I offered the teens an "out." Specifically, I told them that they could pretend to answer the survey, or they could actually fill it out but omit a response to the last question. If they omitted the answer to this question, then I would take this as a signal that they did not want their responses to be included in the research. No student, however, took this option. In every case where parental consent had been obtained, each teen also consented to participate.

In the conduct of research with human subjects, any researcher faces a variety of logistical, methodological, and ethical problems. These problems are even more complicated when the human subjects are minors and when the subject of the research deals with a topic that is personal or potentially embarrassing.

Given all the hurdles associated with conducting research with teens, it is understandable that policy researchers might opt for an approach that obtains information from adults rather than negotiating the extra hurdles of obtaining information directly from minors. For example, researchers could ask teachers, counselors, parents, or other adults who live or work with teens about their perceptions of how teens respond to problems such as teen dating violence. Alternatively, they could ask adults to reflect back on their experiences as teens. Both approaches will generate data about teen dating violence. However, none of the data come from those most closely affected by the problem, that is, from the teens themselves. To formulate good policies and effective programs, at least some of the data need to come from the teens themselves. Although there are clear costs to abandoning a policy researcher's "quick and dirty" approach to data collection, an approach sometimes too readily adopted to meet stringent time constraints, policy research will benefit from the more accurate and robust data that can be gathered from those closest to the problem. Thus, policy analysts must collect data from the teens themselves. They cannot always resort to easily accessible sources of data if the analysis they provide ignores the perspectives of those who are experiencing the problem even as they are experiencing it.

What We Know about Teen Dating Violence

For a number of reasons, there has been little interest and few incentives in collecting data about teen dating violence. The data we do have, however, whether from national data sources, the Internet, or from research on convenience samples of high school students, suggest that teen dating violence exists, takes many forms, is brutal, and can sometimes be lethal.

National databases that report victimization of women have recently become more helpful in identifying the incidence of domestic violence. These databases, however, are not especially helpful in analyzing the magnitude or the characteristics of teen dating violence. They do not tell us about the type of victimization, about whether the victim is a minor, or about whether the victim and the perpetrator had been or are dating partners. As national databases collect more information about the context in which crimes against minors are committed, data will become increasingly useful to those who are interested in understanding the intimate partner violence that affects minors.

While not typically national in scope, the research conducted with small samples of high school and college students is a better source of information about teen dating violence because it reports what teens themselves say about their experiences of violence while dating. The conclusions of these studies, however, vary widely from study to study, in part because of the different ways that researchers define and count the behaviors that constitute dating violence. Moreover, because most of the samples for these studies, including my own, are convenience samples rather than random samples, there is no foundation for making sweeping generalizations about the population of all teens, or even about all minors. What is clear, however, is that despite the variation in the estimates or the inability to generalize broad populations of teens, the incidence of teen dating violence reported in these samples is likely to be underestimated. Moreover, efforts to obtain better data from the teens themselves are complicated by logistical, methodological, and ethical obstacles that can be daunting for policy researchers, especially those who must generate analyses in short periods. Despite these additional complications and time delays, however, we policy researchers should resist the temptation, whenever possible, to substitute second-hand and retrospective self-reports for data generated by those closest to the problem. In the case of teen dating violence, the best data will be generated from among the teens themselves. Chapter Five provides additional data on the issue of teen dating violence from yet one more convenience sample of teens.

CHAPTER 5

EMOTIONALLY ABUSIVE
DATING BEHAVIOR

"'Can I borrow a pencil?' It was the first day of Art I, 4th period. He stuttered as the words came out. I felt sorry for him and I thought about how horrible it must be to live with such an imperfection. I felt so bad about Ramon's stuttering that I decided to ask him out. On our first date we went to the local movie theater. We hit it off immediately. I saw him as a puppy I could take in and care for. I was sure I could change him for the better. Boy, was I wrong."

He had a handicap. She felt sorry for him. She thought she could change him for the better. In many ways, she was just being a compassionate young woman. She was sensitive, kind, helpful, and nurturing. She assumed a role that she thought was appropriate for a young woman in an intimate partner relationship. What motivated her to respond to her partner in this particular way?

Making Frames to Judge Dating Behavior

How a teenage woman judges and responds to her boyfriend's behavior often depends on her perceptions of what her family, her peers, and "society" expect of her. Evaluating the legitimacy of these sources of expectations and mores, and then deciding what is "normal" or healthy, are developmental tasks that must be negotiated by people in any relationship, whether social or work-related. Such tasks, however, can be especially confusing to teenage women new to dating.

In particular, the puzzles they need to solve are numerous. For example, they need to decide how active or passive, or how assertive or submissive they need to be in a dating relationship. To what degree, many wonder, should they be willing to negotiate or forego their own interests, ideas, agendas, or time in order to please their partners? How much "give" is necessary in a healthy relationship? To what extent is it necessary to spend time exclusively with their dating partners, even if it means sacrificing social encounters with family and friends? Should boyfriends always come first? When have their boyfriends' expectations become unrealistic or controlling? To what degree, if any, are teenage women responsible for their boyfriends' retribution when they do not or cannot meet their expectations? Is there ever any good reason why young women should stay in relationships with boyfriends who threaten them or others? In short, what do teenage women have to give up, not only to be accepted but also to be deemed acceptable as a dating partner?

To help young women explore the answers to these questions about what constitutes appropriate dating behaviors, they need to observe, if not turn to, their parents and other family members as models of interpersonal behavior. Peers also set standards about what is "normal" or acceptable in dating relationships. Further, teenage women are influenced by "real-life" media characters whose interactions may model a variety of ways that males and females could relate to each other.

The information from this potpourri of sources is bound to generate inconsistent guidance about what young women should expect in healthy dating relationships. By watching television sitcoms, soap operas, or athletic events, for example, a teenage woman could conclude that love and loyalty mean spending all her free time with a boyfriend and supporting him in all of his activities. To do otherwise could communicate that she is not serious about her relationship with her partner. Conversely, the media may present her with images of strong independent women who work collaboratively with their male and female colleagues and with their dating partners, and who also have crafted interesting lives with and without their partners. Occasionally, the media may feature women who, in contrast to being exploited or dominated by males, actually exploit, dominate, or abuse males. Bombarded by these conflicting messages, or combined with the messages of some of the world's religions that promote a "headship" role for a man and a submissive role for women, it is no wonder that young women can become confused about how to respond to their boyfriends' behaviors.

The story of Alejandra, a young Hispanic woman and now mother of two children, illustrates the dilemmas that young women sometimes confront in the early stages of abusive relationships. As Alejandra describes, she began a relationship with Ramon, a young man whom she thought of "as a puppy she could take care of." She felt sorry for him and was sure "she could change him for the better." After about four months of dating, however, Alejandra became uncomfortable with Ramon's behavior and the expectations he had of her. She also became fearful of how he tried to possess and control her. Subsequently, the relationship turned physically abusive. Alejandra recalls:

> *At first, Ramon was very caring and affectionate. His affection, however, quickly turned to obsession. Ramon never left my sight. And when he did, he always made a point of checking up on me. Ramon became more possessive as the months progressed. I tried to avoid him whenever I could, but it only seemed to make matters worse. He was so controlling. He would escort me to every one of my classes. He made it a point to let everyone know that I was his girlfriend. I was all Ramon had. He rarely associated with his friends, and I rarely associated with mine.*
>
> *If I managed to avoid him in school, then he would spend the afternoon calling my house until I would answer. I would let the phone ring off the wall when I was alone, but I had to answer it as soon as my parents arrived. I thought that if I let the telephone ring, my parents would be upset with me. Ramon was very aware of this. I would plead with him to stop calling. His response was, 'I'm going to keep calling and calling until you talk to me.' Because of my fear, I agreed.*

Alejandra, like many teenage women new to the dynamics of dating, was fairly naïve about Ramon's behaviors. Moreover, although she had dated other boys before, she nevertheless had relatively few personal experiences against which to evaluate Ramon's behaviors. She certainly had less experience than most adult women.

Was it reasonable, she wondered, for Ramon to expect her to be available to him any time he called her, and for as long as he wanted to talk? Was his "escorting" Alejandra to class just the doting attention of a young man taken with his new love, or was it the action of a jealous and possessive young man, and even a potential stalker?

Distinguishing between the negative and positive impacts of such behaviors can be difficult for any woman, especially in the early stages of a relationship. For a teenager, however, the situation can be both confusing and isolating. When Alejandra began to feel fearful and when she began to think that she had caused Ramon's angry outbursts, however, she would have been well advised to heed the clear signs that an emotionally abusive relationship was emerging.

In Chapter Two, I described some of the signs of an emotionally abusive relationship. How frequently and to what degree are teenage women experiencing emotionally abusive behaviors?

Using survey data from 499 female high school juniors and interview data from adult women who had been involved in abusive relationships as teens, this chapter presents data about judgments and experiences of behavior that most would consider emotionally abusive. In addition to illustrating the confusion teens have about what constitutes emotional abuse, the survey data, collected from 392 of the respondents who said they had dated within a year of the survey's administration, show that 22.2 percent report being emotionally abused. The bases for the measurement of these opinions and experiences are indicators commonly identified by domestic violence counselors, court advocates, health care and social workers, and police officers. In particular, these indicators include behaviors that are controlling and isolating, disrespectful, explosive, or threatening.

Experiences of Emotional Abuse

Those who assist adult women who try to separate from abusive situations warn about partners who try to control or isolate them. To what extent do young women fall victim to being controlled or isolated? Irrespective of cultural norms, to what degree have they ceded much of their personal authority to partners who are jealous and possessive, or who engage in stalking? Even as their boyfriends push for exclusive attention, do the young teenage women themselves try to meet expectations—either their own or those of others—that effectively result in isolating them from those best qualified to help and support?

CONTROLLING AND ISOLATING BEHAVIOR

Within the set of controlling and isolating actions are three subsets of behaviors: behaviors that diminish the autonomy and personal authority of teenage women by putting them in submissive positions; behaviors that manifest mistrust; and behaviors that constitute or suggest stalking. Although these specific behaviors do not necessarily lead to a violent dating relationship, most violent dating relationships begin with one or a combination of these behaviors. When a young woman's dating partner exhibits some of these problem behaviors, particularly in the early stages of the relationship, she may be guilty of accepting dangerous dating behaviors, albeit unknowingly. Her behavior may suggest that she is willing to be controlled by her boyfriend, a demeanor that may result in further isolation from others.

To ascertain the extent to which the teenage women in the sample were willing or actually submitted to the controlling and isolating behaviors of their boyfriends, I asked three sets of questions. The first set was designed to measure evidence of autonomy and subservience. The second measured evidence of mistrustful behaviors. The third examined the existence of stalking.

Autonomy and Subservience. Do teenage women think they should get their respective boyfriend's permission before they make plans to go out with other friends? The vast majority (92.9%) strongly disagreed or disagreed that seeking such permission was an expectation they were willing to meet. Specifically, 72.4 percent strongly disagreed and 20.4 percent disagreed that a young woman should seek such permission from her boyfriend before making plans to go out with other friends. By contrast, 7.2 percent either strongly agreed or agreed with the statement, or responded "neither agree nor disagree" or "don't know" to the question.[1]

When asked about the extent to which they thought it appropriate to exclude others from their lives in order to maintain a dating relationship with their boyfriends, most of the teenage women were similarly opposed to meeting such an expectation. Specifically, the vast majority (89%) either strongly disagreed (56.9%) or disagreed (32.1%) that "When dating, a girl should spend less time with her friends." Slightly more than eleven percent (11.1%) held opinions to the contrary or were ambivalent about how to respond.

To examine the experience of ceding or losing autonomy to their dating partners, I asked the young women about the extent to which they collaborated with their boyfriends in deciding what to do on a date. In addition, I asked how frequently their boyfriends objected to their going out without them, a question designed to measure a boyfriend's mistrust of his girlfriend.

A very small percentage of the respondents (1.5%) reported that their boyfriends "never" ask them to help decide what they will do on a date. Almost ten percent (9.8%) of the respondents report that only "once in a while" do their boyfriends ask them to collaborate with them on making dating plans. The vast majority of the sample (90.2%) said their boyfriends "frequently" or "almost always" ask them to help decide what to do on a date.

A measure of behavior that borders on possessiveness and mistrust is the extent to which a boyfriend does not like his girlfriend to go out without him. The majority of the teenage women in the sample (65.8%) said they never experienced this expectation from their boyfriends; 26.9 percent felt this expectation once in a while. For 7.3 percent of the sample, such an expectation was felt frequently (3.4%) or almost always (3.9%).

Mistrust. Whether it is a young woman's choice or her partner's insistence that reduces her autonomy and isolates her from others, a relationship built on mistrust is a major factor in turning a healthy relationship into an abusive one. What percentage of young women in the sample believed their boyfriends

mistrusted them? Did their boyfriends accuse them of lying about almost anything, thus suggesting that they could not be trusted to be "faithful" partners
while remaining friends with other males? Did their boyfriends become angry
when they talked to other boys?

Of 388 respondents, almost three-fourths reported that their boyfriends
never said that they did not trust them. Slightly over 25 percent reported that
their boyfriends said they mistrusted their girlfriends once in a while (19.1%),
frequently (3.9%), or almost always (2.6%). Thus, accusations of mistrust
occur in about one out of five cases. Sixteen percent of the young women reported that their boyfriends accused them of "lying about almost anything"
once in a while. Seven percent (7%), however, reported that they had been accused of lying frequently (3.9%) or almost always (3.1%) in their dealings with
their boyfriends.

According to the teenage women who had dated within the year prior to
the survey, their boyfriends were far more likely to get angry when they
talked with other boys rather than to say they were mistrustful of their partners or accuse them of lying. Specifically, only 35.7 percent of the respondents reported that their boyfriends never became angry when they talked to
other boys. For over 40 percent (42.4%), anger at such behavior occurred
once in a while. For 22 percent of the sample, however, anger was the frequent or usual response when teenage women talked to boys other than their
dating partners.

Stalking. Mistrust of another's partner may manifest itself not only in a
boyfriend's accusations and anger but also in behaviors that attempt to control
his partner's actions. A dating partner may attempt to control his dating
partner's behavior by following his girlfriend around to see what she is doing,
even when she does not welcome such company or behavior.

Some in the sample (7.5%) reported that their boyfriends frequently or almost always had "radar" when it came to things the young teenage women
were doing. For 15.3 percent, this feeling occurred once in a while, whereas
77.2 percent never experienced such intensity in trying to be located by their
boyfriends. While not necessarily unwelcome, almost one third (31.4%) of the
sample said their boyfriends showed up unexpectedly at least once in a while in
places where they were; 4.4 percent reported that their boyfriends showed up
frequently or almost always when they were unexpected.

Although such intense attentiveness may or may not be welcomed by teenage women, the healthiness of such behavior over the long term is certainly
questionable. In general, it suggests that the male partners may be suspicious,
possessive, or controlling. In its extreme, being followed everywhere by a boyfriend, especially when the person being followed resents such behaviors or is

fearful, becomes stalking. With what frequency did the respondents say they experienced stalking?

The vast majority of young women in the sample (91.5%) reported that their boyfriends had never stalked them. Seven percent (7%) had experienced being stalked once in a while. Less than two percent (1.6%) reported being stalked frequently or almost always.

Without the particulars of abuse from those who actually suffered it, statistics are merely numbers on a page. These figures, however, take on more meaning when the stories of the young women who actually suffered abusive teen dating relationships become known. For example, the stories of women like Alissa and Alejandra illustrate the control, the isolation, the mistrust, the jealousy, and the stalking behaviors that typify an emotionally abusive teen dating relationship.

Recall, for example, how Alissa remembered feeling like "she belonged to her new boyfriend Dave." "Nobody leaves me," Dave shouted at her. "Everything centered around Dave," Alissa recalls. Dave was both controlling and possessive, and years passed before Alissa could finally separate from him.

Alejandra was fearful. "Ramon rarely associated with his friends and I rarely associated with mine," she told me. "On one occasion, I managed to spend a few minutes with my friends, only because, fortunately, they were my classmates." Alejandra was isolated, but this was only the beginning of her sad saga with Ramon. In addition to her many efforts to escape his control by lying and putting up a good front with her parents, Alejandra became deeply depressed and withdrawn. She describes how fear, isolation, depression, and despair resulted in an attempted suicide.

> They [her classmates] pleaded with me to leave Ramon, but I would not listen. 'I can't leave him. He needs me,' I would tell them.
>
> My classmates suggested that I apply for the assistant editor position in our school newspaper so I would not spend so much time with Ramon. As news editor of our school paper, I found refuge from Ramon, but as assistant editor, I would have to dedicate myself a lot more to the job than I was currently doing.
>
> I loved being a part of my school newspaper; I have a passion for writing. But in order to qualify for the position, I would have to spend every afternoon working on the paper. When I told Ramon about my plans, he quickly questioned me: 'When are we supposed to spend time together?'
>
> Because of my obligation to Ramon and my lack of dedication to the newspaper, the position was given to someone else. Although I was disappointed, I managed to act nonchalant about it.
>
> It was during this time that I began to feel depressed and withdrawn from

my family. Whenever Ramon was not there, I spent afternoons locked in my bedroom (my parents always thought I was doing my homework). I began to perfect my acting skills, altering my mood when I was with my family. But as soon as I would return to my room, I would cry myself to sleep.

Despite everything, my friends continued to be in contact with me every so often. Candy suggested that I get a job with her at McDonald's downtown, and I quickly agreed. When I asked my parents if I could apply for the job, they agreed 'as long as the job does not affect your grades,' my mom said.

Working at McDonald's was my chance to get away from Ramon. I decided that things had to change and I was going to start with myself. Although new people surrounded me, I was hesitant to make friends. I did not feel I could trust anyone. Candy made it a point to introduce me to everyone. She thought she could introduce me to someone new and I would leave Ramon. After months of frustration, I decided to break off my relationship with Ramon. I tried to end our relationship in the past, but I never managed to escape his control.

Working at McDonald's gave me freedom, but Ramon was losing control of me and he did not like it. Although I had ended our relationship, Ramon continued to pursue me as if nothing had changed. Things between us were getting really out of hand, and I had had enough.

One morning at 7 a.m., the telephone rang. It was Ramon. I told him I did not want to talk to him. He said, 'If you don't talk to me, I'm going to keep calling you.'

Afraid that my parents would wake up, I continued to talk to Ramon. I was due at work at 11 a.m. that morning. It was now 10:45 a.m. and Ramon refused to let me go. Shortly after my father woke up to take me to work, I told him that I was not scheduled to work that day. I was too embarrassed to walk in late, so I decided that lying to my father was my only option.

Because I was scheduled to work but failed to show up, a manager from McDonald's telephoned my home and spoke to my father. My father was upset with me and told me I was irresponsible: 'You cannot be doing these kinds of things when you have a job, Alejandra,' he shouted.

I ran to my room feeling horrible. I decided that this was it. Rather than face my problems, I opted to die. I was tired of Ramon and, because of him, my father was disappointed in me. I slowly opened my bedroom door (Mom was watching television in the living room) and went to my parents' restroom. My mom had some prescription bottles she took to control her pain. I grabbed the first bottle I saw. As I looked into the mirror with tears rolling down my face, I swallowed every single pill in the bottle. . . . tranquilizers. My mom cried all the way to the hospital. . . . 'Young lady,' the nurse said, 'if you had waited a few more minutes before coming here, you would have died.'

Alejandra was scared. She felt alone and trapped. She tried to break up with Ramon but, like many adult women involved in violent domestic relationships, it took her several attempts before she was able to leave her abusive dating partner. Even after she tried to commit suicide, Alejandra continued to see Ramon, always with hope that things would be different.

Young women like Alejandra and Alissa do not always respond to the actions of abusive partners in logical or healthy ways. Instead of confiding in another or seeking other forms of help, they often blame themselves for the troubles in the relationships. Some may even respond by doing things that will "force" themselves into an even closer relationship with their abusive partners. Others avoid confrontation and try to pacify their abusers, lest they lose them. Like Alejandra, they sometimes lie. In general, however, they accede to their boyfriends' expectations when most outside the relationship would consider such expectations inappropriate, if not outrageous. In so doing, they further isolate themselves from those most concerned and able to help.

ATTITUDES TOWARD DISRESPECTFUL BEHAVIORS

Although isolating and controlling behaviors do not necessarily signal the onset of a dating relationship that will become physically or sexually violent, these signs are usually present in the early stages of such violent relationships. When isolating and controlling behaviors accompany another set of behaviors that can, at best, be labeled as disrespectful, then the progression toward physical and sexual abuse is more direct.

Among a potentially long list of disrespectful behaviors, three types were measured in the survey: the experience of being made to wait for one's boyfriend; the experience of a boyfriend's making fun of his dating partner or her family or friends; and being shouted or sworn at.

Being Made to Wait. Illustrative of the disrespect accorded to a young teenage woman is her repeatedly being made to wait for her boyfriend, especially without calling or being given a reason, Alissa describes her high school prom night. That night, her date and his pals "vanished" for over an hour, presumably to park the car. The young women waited for them at the restaurant after the dance.

Although Alissa recalls some humor in the evening, the disrespect Dave and his buddies showed their dates was sadly indicative of their penchant for tending to their own wants and needs first, even when disrespectful or demeaning of others. Moreover, in Dave's case, it signaled other forms of emotional and physical abuse that occurred later in his relationship with Alissa.

That night, Dave and his friends went to the bathroom to smoke dope. I told him he couldn't do that. 'It's my prom!' And I didn't want to get into trouble.
   'It's just one hit,' he said.
   Later, the boys dropped us off in front of the restaurant. Their car broke down and they kept us waiting there, in the rain, for an hour and a half. We had our fake furs on and our hairdos were a mess. We went to White Castle instead.

In contrast to what Alissa described, it would be difficult to find any humor in what happened to Maggie during her relationship with Mark.

   Toward the end of our relationship, Mark would typically cancel plans by leaving notes on my car. On other occasions, he would leave me messages on my answering machine when he knew I was not at home. I cannot count the number of times he would tell me to be somewhere at a certain time, and then he did not show up. He would 'forget.' At other times he would tell me to come over after work, but then, when I showed up, he would close all his windows, turn his air conditioner on full blast, turn his television set up, and turn his lights off so I could not see him. A number of times, I would return home without seeing him because he 'fell asleep' and didn't hear me or hear the phone.

Time and time again, Dave and Mark made Alissa and Maggie wait for them. Repeatedly, each used his girlfriend's time to suit himself. Were such behaviors honest and youthful mistakes made by young men oblivious to norms of etiquette and civility, or were they signs of disrespect and an unwillingness to be accountable for their actions?

At times there is a fine line between making an honest mistake and exhibiting disrespectful behavior. Mindful of this, I asked the young women in the sample to indicate their opinions about the following statement: "If a boyfriend consistently arrives late for a date without calling to say that he will be late, then I think that boyfriend disrespects me." Of those who dated during the past year and responded to the statement, only 13 percent strongly agreed and 35.2 percent agreed that such behavior was disrespectful. Slightly over 17 percent (17.1%) either strongly disagreed (1.8%) or disagreed (15.3%) with this statement. A surprisingly large percentage (34.2%) said they neither agreed nor disagreed with the statement or responded "don't know." Thus, less than half of these teenage women considered such behavior disrespectful. The majority either did not think such behavior was disrespectful or were ambivalent about how to evaluate it.

To what degree did the respondents typically experience being kept waiting, and if they were going to be late, did their boyfriend leave them a message? Slightly over eight percent (8.2%) said their boyfriends never called to leave such a message, and 26 percent said that only once in a while did their boyfriends fail to notify them. The majority (65.7%) reported that their boyfriends did call them if they knew they were going to be late.

Being Stood Up. At the extreme end of making a girlfriend wait for her boyfriend is being stood up for a date. How frequently did the respondents who dated during the past year experience being stood up?

The survey data suggest that being stood up is something that almost one in four women in the sample experienced. Whereas 76.5 percent said they had never been stood up, 20.1 percent said they had been stood up once in a while. For 3.3 percent of the respondents, being stood up by their dates was the norm, whether frequently or almost always.

Some may argue that keeping someone waiting, whether for a social or professional occasion, has become more the norm in recent times. Perhaps, then, the expectation that a boyfriend should not keep his girlfriend waiting is a thing of the past. In an earlier, less hectic and, perhaps, more "chivalrous" era, keeping someone waiting was more difficult to excuse.

While it may be true that being late for appointments or social occasions occurs more frequently and, in this sense, is the "norm," it is not normative in the sense of being acceptable. Being consistently late or keeping someone waiting, even with notification, is unacceptable in most professional relationships. There is even somewhat of a rebellion toward physicians who schedule appointments with their patients and then fail to show up or keep their patients waiting for hours. If this behavior between mere acquaintances is felt to be unacceptable, why, then, would such behavior be acceptable in a social relationship, especially when the parties involved presumably care about each other?

Perhaps being kept waiting somehow elevates the status of a dating partner to that of an individual who is "in demand." This popularity and importance may make his date feel as though he is worth waiting for. Because his time is so valued by others, he deserves her patience and the acceptance of his behavior. In contrast to her partner, her time is not as valuable, so it is perfectly okay to wait for "Mr. Important." After a pattern of being kept waiting ensues, this becomes the acceptable norm within the relationship.

Irrespective of what is normal for many people, psychologists note that making someone wait is a form of passive-aggressive behavior. It is passive in the sense that the aggressor does not actually "do" anything to provoke the behavior. Rather, he fails to do something that is expected so that his aggression is kept covert. A boyfriend who keeps his girlfriend waiting is not actually *doing* something to her. On the contrary, he is covertly taking something precious from her—her time and, perhaps, her sense of self-worth. Further, by making her wait, he is exerting control over how his date uses her time. His behavior reflects a manipulative and selfish personality such that his needs, his time, and his agenda replace hers. Under such conditions, opportunities for healthy collaboration, accountability, and commitment are virtually impossible.

Hurtful Teasing. In addition to behaviors that communicate disrespect, the ways individuals speak to each other can also communicate whether the parties in the relationship respect each other. For example, in a healthy intimate partner relationship, the partners do not usually make fun of each other to hurt, demean, or embarrass each other. Nor do they engage in hurtful teasing of families or friends.

Teasing and making fun of others can be funny and harmless. However, when a boyfriend makes comments designed to hurt his partner, whether about her dress, her mannerisms, or her appearance, or when a girlfriend asks her boyfriend to stop making such comments because they hurt, then teasing and wisecracks cease to be funny. Moreover, they are often evidence of disrespect.

To assess the extent to which hurtful teasing and other forms of verbal putdowns are experienced by teenage women involved in dating relationships, I asked the survey respondents to report how frequently they thought their boyfriends tried to hurt them by making fun of them when they were alone. Over seventy percent (71.1%) said their boyfriends never tried to hurt them by making fun of them when they were alone, and 25.3 percent reported that this happened once in a while. Only 3.7 percent indicated that their boyfriends frequently or almost always hurt them by making fun of them when they were alone.

In contrast to the percentages of those who reported that their boyfriends made fun of them when they were alone, the percentages of teenage women who said their boyfriends frequently or almost always made fun of them in front of their friends was slightly less. Specifically, 2.6 percent reported that their boyfriends frequently or almost always made fun of them in front of their friends compared to 3.7 percent who exhibited such behavior when the partners were alone; 25.8 percent indicated that such behavior happened once in a while, and 71.6 percent said their boyfriends never made fun of them in front of their friends.

While fairly few young women experienced hurtful teasing, whether alone with their boyfriends or in front of their friends, the percentages of teenage women who reported that their boyfriends teased their friends were substantially higher. For example, whereas roughly half (50.1%) of the respondents said their boyfriends never made fun of their friends, 40.3 percent said this behavior occurred once in a while. Almost 10 percent (9.5%) reported that their boyfriends frequently (7.2%) or almost always (2.3%) made fun of their friends. Thus, the young women reported that their boyfriends tease their friends more than they are themselves teased by their boyfriends.

Although teasing was common among the teens, most young women reported that their boyfriends seldom made fun of family members. Specifically, the data show that 80.6 percent of the sample reported that such behavior never occurred, and 16.8 percent indicated that their boyfriends made fun of family members once in a while. Only 2.6 percent reported that their boyfriends frequently or almost always made fun of family members. Why the difference when it comes to making fun of family members?

Perhaps the male partners felt that making fun of their girlfriends' friends was "macho" and would not get them into too much trouble. By contrast, making fun of their partners' family members may be considered so disrespectful that it could result in a break-up.

Being Sworn and Shouted At. Even more disrespectful than keeping a partner waiting or teasing her in hurtful ways is shouting into the face of one's girlfriend, swearing at her, or calling her obscene or hurtful names. These behaviors, which often accompany outbursts of anger, are disrespectful, demeaning, and embarrassing. Further, if they occur frequently, especially after a young woman has objected to such treatment, these actions can be particularly devastating because they can erode a young woman's self-esteem. Recalling the stories of Maggie, Alejandra, and Alissa illustrates the connection between being demeaned and the lack of self-esteem.

"During one conversation,'" Maggie told me, he [Mark] "yelled at me and called me a 'bitch' while on the phone with a friend." Another time, after trying to collect some loans she had made to Mark, Maggie discovered that Mark had been lying to her about his financial condition. "He called me names at the top of his voice," Maggie remembered.

Alejandra said that Ramon made her "feel horrible." He would embarrass her in front of people by saying "You're so stupid. Just look at you," he would yell. "I would just stand there in dismay, swallowing every word," Alejandra said. The tone of his voice and the frequency of these outbursts left little doubt that Ramon was not simply kidding around or teasing Alejandra.

Alissa's story is even more dramatic and illustrative of an extreme form of disrespect and emotional abuse. "We would get invited out and he'd say we couldn't go. He'd be pushing or shoving or flipping tables. He was big on coming right up into my face and yelling and telling me that I should understand what he was capable of doing to me." When they did go out, Alissa recalled, "Dave would get very drunk and say things that were embarrassing or hurtful to our hosts. I lived in terror of what he would say to people." In the context of shoving, pushing, or throwing tables, Dave's yelling and threats made it clear his intent was neither light nor playful. He had clearly stepped far over the line into emotional abuse. Moreover, his behavior, far from respectful, began to signal the onset of physical abuse. Dave's behavior was so toxic that Alissa became convinced that she was insane. What else could explain the agoraphobia that she had developed after they had married? What else could explain why Dave was so cruel to her? Alissa's self-esteem was at rock bottom, and Dave's emotional abuse was the primary agent of the rockslide.

Were there many young women in the sample who experienced disrespect and emotional abuse in the form of being shouted and sworn at? In the survey, almost 90 percent (89.4%) reported that their boyfriends had never sworn at them; 8.8 percent, however, said that such outbursts occurred once in a while. Very few of the respondents (1.9%) had frequent experiences of boyfriends shouting in their faces.

Were young women called unflattering names? Yes. Young teenage women reported being called unflattering names once in a while (29.4%), frequently (5.4%), or almost always (.5%). The 64.7 percent who reported that they had never been called unflattering names by their boyfriends is substantially lower than the 89 percent of the sample who reported that they never experienced being shouted or sworn at by their boyfriends. Although they may not like it, 13 percent said they would keep dating a boyfriend who swore frequently at them. Additionally, 25.8 percent were ambivalent about how they would react to such behavior. Thus, while 61.2 percent of the sample strongly disagreed (26.5%) or disagreed (34.7%) that they would keep dating a boy who swears at them frequently, over one third did not clearly disapprove of or were willing to tolerate such behavior.

Consistently being made to wait, being demeaned, or being sworn at can be a hurtful experience for anyone. The experience of these behaviors, however, can be devastating and corrosive to the self-esteem of young women who are still in their formative years. Moreover, the context, tone, and frequency of such encounters may ultimately convince a teenage woman that her partner's comments are correct. She has misbehaved. She has done something to embarrass him. She deserves to be chastised for her behavior. Furthermore, she may believe her boyfriend has the right to punish her. When these behaviors occur in the context of conflicts or angry outbursts, if they occur frequently, or if the tone is obviously derisive and intended to put the young teenage woman "in her place," then it is unlikely that the fault lies with the young woman. Unfortunately, many teenagers do not seem to understand this.

ANGER

Isolating and controlling or disrespectful behaviors can derive from feelings of anger or can be a prelude to angry outbursts. As described earlier, a young woman may be accused of "misbehaving" or violating some spoken or unspoken norm or expectation that her boyfriend has of her. For example, she should not talk to other boys, or she should be available to her boyfriend at all times. Furthermore, she may be accused of responding improperly or insufficiently to his sexual overtures. Perhaps she "makes" her boyfriend angry by confronting him when he keeps her waiting or makes plans for dates without consulting her, or complains that she is not paying enough attention to him. In such situations, a boyfriend may become angry, often unexpectedly, sometimes intensely, and may occasionally resort to physical violence directed at objects or the dating partner herself.

The survey data suggest that perhaps more than any other behavior, anger is prevalent in many teen dating relationships. Although 37.1 percent reported that their boyfriends never became angry with them and 52.3 percent said their boyfriends became angry only once in a while, 10.5 percent reported that anger was the norm and that their boyfriends frequently (7.7%) or almost always (2.8%) became angry with them.

Of these same respondents, what percentage reported that their boyfriends became angry *easily* with them? Almost 24 percent (23.8%) reported that their boyfriends became angry easily once in a while, and 7.2 percent reported that their boyfriends became angry easily frequently.

To what extent did the respondents say their boyfriends got violent when they were angry? Slightly over six percent (6.2%) reported that their boyfriends frequently or almost always got violent when they became angry; 14.7 percent said that violence accompanied their boyfriends' anger once in a while; 2.1 percent said that when their boyfriends became angry, there was almost always some violence that accompanied it.

Because of the publicity given to the inappropriate expressions of anger, for example, when a teen goes on a shooting rampage, or when someone engages in road rage, it is easy to overlook the extent to which anger and violence may be present in teen dating relationships. What cannot be overlooked, however, is how pervasive anger is in present-day relationships, whether at school, in the work place, or among intimate partners who are only teens.

THREATS

In the cycle of teen dating violence, emotionally abusive behaviors can sometimes become more than controlling, isolating, disrespectful, or explosive. Such behaviors can also become life-threatening. While many women are willing to tolerate being sworn at, will they draw the line at threats of physical harm?

Maggie's story suggests that the answer is "No." She continued to date Mark even after he had made several verbal threats against her or toward himself. Given the context in which Mark made these threats, it would be difficult not to feel fear or to take his threats seriously.

The first occasion when Maggie recalled Mark making threatening remarks occurred after Maggie and Mark had "made up" from an earlier fight—a fight that had made Mark so angry that "he punched the steering wheel and his car window so hard that he broke two of his knuckles." According to Maggie, Mark then ran out of the car across a very busy main street, without looking, and "disappeared for half an hour."

"I went inside and told my roommate what had happened. And then I knew I could not end it with him because he seemed to care so much. When he returned, we talked. We made up." Is it possible that Maggie and her peers think that a boyfriend's threat to harm himself indicates a genuine concern for the dating relationship?

> *The next morning, I told Mark that I could never feel as secure with him again. This seemed to set him off. In my room, there was a window shade that anyone who had ever been to my apartment had signed. Mark said he wanted to write something on it. He made me leave the room. When I walked back into the room expecting to see something very romantic, I read a short sentence. It said I would not have to worry about anything any more because he would not be around after that day. . . .*

Whether part of a sudden outburst of anger or a calculated effort to warn or intimidate a person, leveling threats against another or oneself clearly signals the existence of an abusive relationship. Further, making such threats is often the bridge between emotional abuse and physical or sexual abuse.

More than occasionally, when threats begin to fly, a boyfriend may threaten himself with physical harm, as we saw with Mark. Although 86.8 percent of the teenage women who dated during the past year never heard their boyfriends make a threat to hurt themselves, 13.2 percent of the sample did hear their boyfriends threaten to hurt themselves. For 9.8 percent of the sample, such threats occurred once in a while. However, for 3.4 percent, these threats were common and occurred frequently or even more often.

Did the sample respondents worry that their boyfriends would hurt them if they tried to break up? The vast majority (91.5%) never entertained such worries. Slightly over two percent (2.1%), however, worried about this frequently or almost always when they were with their boyfriends; 6.5 percent had this worry once in a while.

An extreme form of threat-making is the threat to kill one's partner if she wants to break up. Virtually none of the respondents (98.2%) said their boyfriends ever threatened murder if they wanted to break up. Of the 387 respondents, however, 1.3 percent or five young women heard their boyfriends make these threats once in a while or frequently.

If not threatened with murder explicitly, did their partners' behaviors ever make the teenage women fear their boyfriends would hurt them physically? Almost three-fourths of the respondents said they never felt this way. However, 22.4 percent said that once in a while, they thought their boyfriends might hurt them physically, and 3.6 percent said they felt this way frequently (2.3%) or almost always (1.3%).

How many and to what extent did any of the respondents agree that a girl should keep dating a boy who threatens her? Almost 90 percent (89%) strongly agreed (56.3%) or agreed (32.7%) that a teenage woman should *not* keep dating a boyfriend who verbally threatens her; 6.6 percent were ambivalent about how to respond to the question; but 4.4 percent or 17 students strongly disagreed (2.6%) or disagreed (1.8%). In other words, 17 respondents believed that a teenage woman should keep dating a boyfriend who verbally threatens her.

In addition to being verbally threatened, young women are sometimes threatened by boyfriends who drive fast to scare them. Although 77.8 percent of the respondents said their boyfriends never did this, 18.6 percent said their male partners engaged in this form of risky or threatening behavior at least once in a while. For 4.6 percent of the sample, such behaviors were common. Specifically, 2.3 percent of the young teenage women said their boyfriends frequently drove fast to scare them, and 1.3 percent of the sample, or five young women, reported that their boyfriends almost always drove fast to scare them.

When threatening behaviors begin to surface in a teen dating relationship, physical and sexual abuse are often not far behind. Threats may become the transition between emotionally violent and physically abusive behavior. At first, abuse may be directed toward objects or animals. Later, its object may be a dating partner with a name like Maggie, Alissa, or Alejandra.

In most relationships, there are probably occasions when mistakes and misunderstanding cause hurt, pain, or anger for either or both of the dating partners. Being hurt by or becoming angry with a dating partner does not necessarily suggest or predict a physically or sexually abusive relationship. However, behaviors that are disrespectful, designed to control or isolate another, or result in damage to objects or injury to people or animals, are signs of an emotionally abusive relationship.

How can these intentions be evaluated so that a young woman can discern the difference between the harmless mistakes or expressions of emotions of a smitten boyfriend and the actions of a seriously manipulative, unhealthy, or threatening partner? An analysis of Alissa's story suggests three factors for helping young teenage women interpret the difference. Specifically, the context, the frequency, and the tone of the behaviors provide a framework to assist young women in understanding the intent of their boyfriends' behaviors.

While Alissa recalls the event somewhat humorously, the evening of her senior prom was the wrong occasion for her boyfriend to make her wait for him in the pouring rain. The context of this action can only mean that it was intentionally disrespectful and controlling. In a once-in-a-lifetime context of a senior prom, the boys' behavior could only be construed as selfish and manipulative. For those who experienced such treatment more than once, the frequency suggests nothing but disrespect. Moreover, if the exchanges are accompanied by shouting or derisive tones, then the behaviors have clearly crossed the line from playfulness or mistakes into emotional abuse.

When a teenage woman is puzzled by her boyfriend's behavior, either because it is foreign to her or even bizarre, or when she cannot achieve the emotional distance from him to reflect properly on the context, frequency, and tone of his behaviors, then she is likely to be confused about what is happening in her dating relationship. In these circumstances, a young woman is well advised to pay attention to her first instincts and feelings. If she feels disrespected, embarrassed, or fearful, if she begins to dread seeing her boyfriend because his behavior is unpredictable or explosive, or if she finds herself alone and without friends because he never leaves her alone, then she probably is being "dissed." She should probably be fearful, and she should probably get away.

Developing intimate relationships does not give a boyfriend the license to make all the decisions or to dictate how his girlfriend uses her time, how she should dress, or with whom she should associate. Such behaviors are mistrustful and jealous. Intimacy does not result from mistrust or jealousy, nor can a partnership develop when two people do not trust each other. Thus, when a young woman feels emotionally abused, she probably is being emotionally abused. Indeed, the data suggest there is a statistically significant correlation ($p=.05$, two-tailed, $n=380$) in the "right" direction between a respondent's saying she has been emotionally abused and specific indicators of emotional abuse. That is, as the number of people who report having been emotionally abused increases, so too does the frequency of having experienced virtually every indicator of emotional abuse.[2] However, despite the majority's having the knowledge to recognize emotional abuse when they experience it, the frequency distributions also suggest that many young teenage women do not recognize emotional abuse as such.

CHAPTER 6

PHYSICALLY AND SEXUALLY
ABUSIVE BEHAVIOR

"Suppose you have been dating a guy for about three months. You have sex with him. You date him a few more times, but then you break up. About a month later, you are invited to a party at a friend's house. Your ex-boyfriend has not been invited, but he shows up anyway. In the middle of the party, your 'ex' enters the house uninvited, finds you, grabs you by the hair, and pulls you into the yard. You are stunned, but you struggle to get away from him. But he is stronger than you and, after all, he is yanking you by the hair, which really hurts. He throws you down on the ground, pins you down by the shoulders, and has sex with you. Have you been raped?"

I n posing this question to a group of high school students, a noted domestic violence counselor and author of a popular book on teen dating violence, did not intend to be provocative.[1] Sadly, however, she was. Instead of getting nods of agreement to what she thought was a rhetorical question— "Yes, of course I was raped!"—the classroom of young teenage women broke into an animated discussion. "Was it rape? That's a good question. Was it?"

These teens were debating the answer to a question that should have been obvious: Forced sex is rape. If "common sense" did not tell this to the teens, then the law surely would. Even if a young woman is not a virgin, forced sex is rape. Even if the two people involved know each other casually or, perhaps, had even dated before, forced sex is rape. Even in cases where the partners are married, forced sex is rape. Even when there is mutual "consent," sexual activity with a minor female, depending on the age of the perpetrator, can be construed as aggravated sexual assault or even criminal sexual assault.

However, these young women were not sure about whether the young woman described by Mrs. Clarke had been raped. After all, hadn't the girl previously had sex with this man? Don't you have to be a virgin to be raped? Once you have had sex, surely you are "damaged goods" and incapable of being sexually molested, especially by someone you had dated previously. The classroom debate continued.

How prevalent is this confusion among teenage women? What constitutes young women's attitudes concerning appropriate or inappropriate, or even unlawful, dating behavior?

Physically Violent Dating Behavior

Has physically abusive dating behavior escalated significantly in teen dating relationships or is it possible that teens and researchers are mislabeling youthful mistakes and excesses for signs of an emotionally abusive relationship? When teens have had something thrown at them, been shoved, been held against their wills, been punched, or been beaten, these actions cannot be misinterpreted as love or concern. Moreover, such behaviors cannot be excused, even if a young woman believes she inadvertently provoked her boyfriend into such behaviors.

Alejandra first experienced physical abuse when she and Ramon were arguing over "something frivolous."

> *All of a sudden, he grabbed my arm and squeezed with all his strength. I told him to stop and he wouldn't until I did what he said. After the incident, I thought I was at fault and I excused his behavior by saying to myself, 'It's all right because he really loves me.' Then, in front of my friends, he pinched me.*

After several attempts to break up with Ramon, he still loomed as a threat to her. Was it possible that Alejandra was confused and thought that when Ramon was "driven" to use *extreme* behavior with her, it was a sign of the *extreme* love he had for her, a love so strong that he could not hold back his emotions? Alejandra's friends informed school officials of the threat Ramon posed to Alejandra. Despite being protected by school officials, who had ordered Ramon to stay away from Alejandra, Alejandra found that after she left school, such protection was insufficient in helping her to feel safe. It was then that the physical abuse began to escalate.

> *No one was around to protect me and, for some unknown reason, school officials had not informed my parents about what was going on. Ramon continued to accompany me home. 'You're never going to be able to get rid of me,' he would say. I felt hopeless and he knew it.*

> *One afternoon, I told him he had to leave early because my mother did not want him to stay (an excuse I thought of spontaneously). He became angry and said, 'I'm not leaving here until 5 o'clock.' I became frustrated with him and told him to leave. He stood up and pulled my hair. That is when I decided to fight back. I was tired of this treatment and did not want to tolerate his abusive behavior any more. I pushed him away and he grabbed my arm and bit it so hard it began to bleed.*

After experiencing the extent of her boyfriend's rage many times, and feeling that she was being stalked rather than "accompanied," Alejandra began to become a victim of physical abuse. Despite the increasing fear she felt, Alejandra refused to tell her parents, and the school failed to inform them of her predicament. Did school officials feel that they would be overstepping their bounds legally or would possibly be violating a student's privacy and trust? Whatever their thinking, Alejandra continued to live in constant fear of abuse.

Maggie also watched emotional abuse slip into physical violence. The violence that was previously directed toward the car, when Mark broke two knuckles, later became violence directed toward his girlfriend. Maggie's vivid recollection from Chapter One illustrates her increasing problems.

> *Hanging up the phone after being highly irritated, [Mark] grabbed his [motor] bike and I was told to wait for him. Then he got crazy. He told me I was lucky that I was his girlfriend, or he would have thrown me over the balcony. He then told me that if I did not move, he would 'plow right over me' with his bike.*

Mark's behavior is a prime example of displaced anger. He could not very well reach into the phone and deal with the source of his anger. Conversely, Maggie was conveniently close at hand to receive his emotional and physical outburst.

For Alissa, physical abuse was frequent, varied, and potentially lethal. A survivor of 30 years of abuse which began when she was 18 years old and continued with the same man until she was 48, Alissa details a series of increasingly violent incidents which began when she was a teenager and continued into adulthood.

- *"I caught a black eye when I tried to break up a fight."*
- *"I don't know what I said or did one day, but he came up behind me and slapped me across the head from behind. He knocked me straight off the chair."*
- *"I'd be on the floor (I was pregnant) and he'd be kicking me. I'd be cradling the baby and he'd be kicking me in the back."*

- "*The abuse became so bad that my two kids were telling me to get him out of the house. He would go after the boys with such force you'd be afraid he wouldn't stop. I'd have to punch and kick him to get him off the kids. I was the physical barrier between him and the kids.*"

- "*One night, he didn't want me to do something. He cracked me so hard his hand print was still on my face.*"

- "*The night he beat me, it was Mother's Day. I was black and blue all over.*"

- "*The day before I planned to move out, Dave went berserk. That day was completely brutal and I will never forget it. He had me cornered. I couldn't get to the phone. He had me by the hair and was trying to pull it off and scalp me. I flew into walls. Then it was a blur.*"

How is it that women persist in such relationships, even to the point of marrying someone who had been abusive when they were dating as teens? The survey data suggest at least a partial answer to this question: Young teenage women do not view some patently physically abusive behaviors either as abusive or as something to be avoided. For example, when asked to respond to the statement, "I wouldn't keep dating a boyfriend who kicks me," only 77.6 percent strongly agreed (62.8%) or agreed (14.8%). Almost 13 percent (12.8%) of the respondents strongly disagreed (9.2%) or disagreed (3.6%) that they would cease dating a boyfriend who kicks them, and 9.7 percent neither agreed nor disagreed with the statement.

When asked to react to the statement "If a boyfriend threw something at me while we were dating, I would think it no big deal," the respondents were more reticent to accept this type of physically abusive behavior. Specifically, 83.7 percent either strongly disagreed (48.7%) or disagreed (34.9%) with the statement. However, 11.5 percent neither agreed nor disagreed, whereas 4.3 percent agreed and .5 percent strongly agreed with the statement. Thus, in their thinking about behaviors such as having a boyfriend throw something at them, 16.3 percent of the respondents were either ambivalent about or unwilling to think of this behavior as something significant or important.

If the physical violence escalates to the point where a boyfriend punches his girlfriend, do the respondents think that the girl should break up with him immediately? Almost 65 percent (64.8%) strongly agree that a girl should immediately break up with a boyfriend who punches her while 18.4 percent agree. Eleven percent of the respondents, however, were ambivalent about how to respond to such behavior, neither agreeing nor disagreeing that such behavior should be rejected. Slightly over three percent (3.1%) disagreed and 2.8 percent strongly disagreed that a young woman should immediately break up with a boyfriend who punches her.

Although the vast majority of young teenage women who responded to the survey showed good judgment in their theoretical rejections of a boyfriend's physically abusive behavior, a surprisingly high number of respondents were either willing to tolerate such behavior or were ambivalent about how to respond to it. In conducting informal polls with high school students whom he has addressed about teen dating violence, Tom Santoro found that a girl's willingness to tolerate abusive behavior increased in direct proportion to the amount of time the couple had been dating. Tom posed two scenarios to a gathering of young women that illustrate this point.

> *Much to your delight, Mr. Perfect has just asked you out for a date. He is good looking. He is charming. He made a good impression on your parents. And now, you are on your way to a Beastie Boys concert. On the way to the concert, you reach for the CD player and, in doing so, knock over the remains of a lukewarm cappuccino that was in the cup holder next to you. The contents spill all over the dashboard and onto the floor. Your date then slams on the brakes, pulls over to the side of the road, and begins to scream at you at the top of his voice. He grabs you by the hair, pulls you toward him, and stares straight into your face. 'You stupid bitch,' he mumbles. 'You stupid bitch.'*

"How many of you would go on another date with this guy?" Tom asked the classroom of young women before him. "Please raise your hands."

Almost no one raised her hand. However, when Tom changed the scenario, describing this incident not as part of the first date but having occurred after three months of dating, approximately 75 percent of the students raised their hands to indicate they would continue dating this type of boyfriend. Why?

These scenarios and the survey questions about what teenage women would do if confronted with such behaviors, were hypothetical. How many respondents actually experienced being kicked or being punched? Of the 386 survey respondents who said they had dated within a year of the administration of the survey, 5.7 percent reported that they had experienced physical abuse. What other forms of physical violence do young teenage women experience while dating? With what degree of abuse are they living? For example, to what degree do the respondents report being pulled by the hair? Being shoved? Being held down by the shoulders during a fight? Being bruised or bitten? Being wrestled with roughly? Being physically stopped when they wanted to drive away or walk away from their boyfriend? Or having their boyfriends drive fast in order to scare them? The survey data suggest that the majority of teenage women who have dated recently have not experienced these behaviors. However, as many as 34 percent have experienced one or more of these behaviors at least once in a while.

BEING KICKED

The vast majority (97.4%) of teenage women in the sample have never had the experience of being kicked by their boyfriends. For 1.6 percent of the sample, being kicked by a boyfriend occurred once in a while. One percent of the sample had been kicked frequently or almost always during encounters with their boyfriends.

BEING PUNCHED

Similarly, 95.1 percent of the respondents reported that their boyfriends never punched them. However, almost five percent (4.9%) or 19 respondents reported that their boyfriends punched them once in a while. None of the respondents reported that their boyfriends frequently or almost always punched them when they were together.

BEING PULLED BY THE HAIR

Almost 95 percent (94.6%) of the teenage women in the sample reported that their boyfriends had never pulled them by the hair while 4.7 percent of the respondents reported they experienced such behavior once in a while. Slightly less than one percent (.8%) of the sample reported that they frequently or almost always experienced such behaviors.

BEING SHOVED

The experience of being shoved by a boyfriend is an occasional-to-common occurrence for 10.9 percent of the young women in the sample. Although 89.1 percent reported that their boyfriends never shoved them, 8.5 percent reported that shoving occurred once in a while. For 2.4 percent, being shoved occurred frequently (2.1%) or almost always (.3%) when they were with their boyfriends.

BEING HELD DOWN BY THE SHOULDERS

Most of the teenage women in the sample (91.2%) reported that they had never had the experience of being held down by the shoulders by their boyfriends during a fight. Eight percent, however, reported that they had experienced such force once in a while. For .8 percent, the experience was common and occurred frequently or almost always when they and their boyfriends have had a disagreement.

BEING BRUISED OR BITTEN

The majority of respondents to the survey (85.5%) reported that they had never been bruised or bitten by their boyfriends when dating. However, 11.9 percent said this occurred once in a while and 2.6% reported that being bruised or bitten by a boyfriend was a common experience that occurred frequently or almost always when they were dating.

BEING WRESTLED WITH ROUGHLY

Although "playful" wrestling between partners is often a common prelude to other forms of intimate activity, physical abuse occurs when an individual is being wrestled with so roughly that it is painful and one of the partners asks the other to stop. Almost 80 percent (79.6%) of the young teenage women in the sample reported that they never experienced such behavior while dating. In contrast, 17.5 percent said that their boyfriends wrestled roughly with them once in a while, while 2.9 percent reported that such an experience was common, occurring frequently (2.1%) or almost always (.8%).

DRIVING FAST TO SCARE

Almost 78 percent (77.8%) of the respondents reported that their boyfriends never drove fast with the intent to scare them. For 22.2 percent of the sample, however, this tactic was adopted by their boyfriends at least once in a while (18.6%), frequently (2.3%), or almost always (1.3%).

BEING PHYSICALLY STOPPED

The most frequent physically abusive behavior reported by the young women in the sample was the experience of being physically stopped by their boyfriends when they wanted to walk away. Almost 28 percent (27.9%) experienced this behavior once in a while. For 6.2 percent of the sample, being physically stopped when they wanted to walk away occurred frequently (3.9%) or almost always (2.3%).

The survey participants relied on their particular frames of reference to respond to questions that measured their experience with specific forms of physical abuse. With regard to the frequency of occurrence of each type of physical abuse surveyed, the incidence of occurrence in the "once in a while" or "often" categories increased in direct proportion to the less violent nature of the action. Wrestling, driving fast, and physically stopping the girlfriend from leaving occurred more frequently. Conversely, the more intimate and more physically harmful actions of bruising and biting, pinning down, shoving, hair pulling, punching, and kicking were experienced less frequently.

With regard to the less outwardly violent actions, perhaps the young women's experience with wrestling was of a more playful nature and being stopped from walking away from their boyfriend was construed as his caring so much for her that it almost seemed flattering. Could driving fast simply be a display of his macho nature? It also seems likely that these less violent actions would be kept hidden between the two partners, whereas bruises, kicks, punches, and bite marks could be difficult to hide. If one believes that an individual who uses his superior strength to abuse a partner has lower self-esteem, then perhaps these young men employ these more visible forms of physical abuse less often because they fear being "found out." Such behaviors could be "safer," still prove a point, and exert power and control over their dating partner without being as physically blatant.

The data from the survey suggest that while the majority of respondents have not experienced physical violence and are not inclined to tolerate it, a substantial number (5.7%) of teenage women have experienced some forms of physical violence. Moreover, even larger numbers of young women are willing to tolerate abusive behavior or are ambivalent about how to respond to it.

Does one's racial or ethnic background suggest a relationship to physically abusive dating relationships? The data suggest the answer is "Yes," but the answer is not as clear as the data suggest. For example, in contrast to the statistically insignificant relationship between emotional abuse and race, there is a statistically significant relationship between physical abuse and race (χ^2=15.828, d.f. 3, p=.001). Specifically, the "other" race category, which includes Native Americans, Pacific Islanders, nonwhite Hispanics, Alaskans, and Asians, and the category of Hispanics, reported higher percentages of physical abuse than either African Americans or whites. In particular, 20.6 percent of "other" race respondents reported experiencing physical abuse, in contrast to 6 percent of Hispanics, 3.9 percent of African Americans, and 3.8 percent of whites. These statistics contrast with other research that says that the experience of physical violence is equally common to all races.[2]

Sexually Abusive Behavior

If young teenage women are not strongly inclined to break up with boyfriends who emotionally or physically abuse them, then will they draw the line at sexually abusive behaviors? What are young women's perceptions about what is sexually appropriate and inappropriate behavior in a dating relationship?

The survey data suggest that the difference between what young teenage women *think they will tolerate* and the degree to which they *actually will tolerate* sexually abusive behavior, is striking. Further, teenage women seem very confused about what types of sexual activity constitute abuse or even rape.

For example, in asking the young teenage women in the survey to respond to the hypothetical question "If a boyfriend gets pushy about having sex, I would break up with him," almost 13 percent (12.8%) either strongly disagreed (1.5%) or disagreed (11.3%). Additionally, 36.1 percent neither agreed nor disagreed with the statement. Only 23.5 percent strongly agreed and 27.6 percent agreed. Thus, almost half of the sample (48.8%) indicated either ambivalence or disagreement about the notion of whether a young teenage woman should break up with a boyfriend who got "pushy" about having sex.

Although the intent of the question was clear when it was constructed, at the time the survey was administered it was obvious that there were some ambiguous terms in this question. For example, "pushy" behaviors could range from a boyfriend's consistently stating his desire to have sex to being physically aggressive or even violent in forcing a woman to engage in sexual activities. Further, even the phrase "have sex" has taken on new meanings. For example, research has shown that teenagers think that intercourse is the only way to "have sex." They do not consider sexual behaviors such as anal penetration, mutual masturbation, or oral sex as "having sex."[3]

In contrast to the hypothetical situation, how many in the sample actually experienced their boyfriends getting pushy about having sex? Over 80 percent (80.6%) said this never happened with their boyfriends. For 14 percent, this was their experience once in a while. For 5.4 percent, however, such was their experience frequently (2.8%) or almost always (2.6%).

A somewhat stronger hypothetical situation was offered for consideration to the survey respondents. This time, I substituted the phrase "forced me to have sex against my will" for "gets pushy about having sex." In this case, 3.8 percent of the respondents indicated that they either strongly disagreed (2.8%) or disagreed (1.0%) that they would break up with a boyfriend who forced them to have sex against their will. Almost 10 percent (9.7%) neither agreed nor disagreed that breaking up is a good action to take when a boyfriend forces a young woman to have sex against her will. In effect, 13.5 percent of the sample indicated ambivalence about or disagreement with the idea that they should break up with someone who had raped them. The rest of the sample, 86.5 percent, would not keep dating a boyfriend who, because it was forced, effectively raped them. Moreover, most of the sample (95.9%) reported that they had never been forced to have sex with their boyfriends. For 3.9 percent of the young teenage respondents, being forced to have sex against their wills occurred once in a while, and one respondent (.3%) said that this was frequently her experience when she was with her boyfriend.

Whether forced to have sex or having experienced other forms of sexual abuse, how many respondents reported that they had been sexually abused by a boyfriend? The data suggest that a minority thought they had been sexually abused (5.4%). The vast majority, 94.6 percent, reported that they had never been sexually abused.

Did this abuse vary by race or ethnicity? In general, the survey data indicate that there is no statistically significant relationship between one's race and the level of sexual violence experienced by those who dated within a year of the survey's administration. Young teenage white women, however, reported the highest percentage of sexual abuse within their racial category, 6.9 percent, compared to other groups that ranged between 2 percent (African American) and 3 percent (Hispanic).

Although the majority of respondents were inclined to be intolerant of sexually abusive behaviors, a sizable minority were either willing to tolerate these behaviors or were ambivalent about how to respond to them. Sadly, in their struggles to come to grips with their ambivalent feelings about specific sexual behaviors, societal norms were not very helpful. In theory, for example, this country allows women to have control over their bodies and to say "No" to those who want to use their bodies for sex against their wills. In reality, while the law upholds a woman's right to protect her body, the judicial system often dismisses the action of the offender by ascribing guilt to the woman for the sexual misconduct of the other.

The results of this research—that young teenage women are very confused about what constitutes abuse, especially sexual abuse—should be especially disturbing for parents, teachers, and counselors. Young women lack frames of reference, life experience, and role models that will help them distinguish between healthy, exploitative, marginally abusive, or very abusive sexual behaviors. Although the vast majority are not experiencing the varied forms of physical abuse of a truly harmful or lethal nature, they do not seem to understand the seriousness of the threat that typically accompanies less outwardly harmful actions such as reckless driving, wrestling roughly, and stopping them when they want to go, either through intimidation or through the use of physical force.

Just as "less harmful" drugs such as marijuana do not always lead to stronger addictive drugs, less violent actions do not always lead to more violent behaviors such as kicking, bruising, biting, or punching. However, like most who become addicted to hard drugs after experimenting with "lighter" narcotics, men who become brutally violent in a dating relationship do not generally begin with brutality but with less violent forms of abuse that could, at least, surely be deemed disrespectful or exploitative.

Most young teenage women cannot imagine that disrespectful or marginally violent behaviors may ever escalate to extreme physical or sexual brutality. Indeed, many who experience less violent forms of abuse may never need to confront a dating partner who hits, kicks, shoves, or forces sex on them. The trouble is that it is difficult for young teenage women to tell whether the violence will escalate. Because the consequences can be so grave, however, parents, teachers, counselors, and others who work closely with young teenage women must warn them of the possibilities and share information that, in no uncertain terms, is graphic in detail, explains what happens when physical and sexual abuse occur, and shows how these behaviors differ from "playfulness" or "getting carried away."

CHAPTER 7

FINDING A WAY OUT

"As I look back at the things I went through with Ramon, I am glad that I decided to end our relationship. My parents supported me through it all and acted on my behalf. They never questioned the accusations I made about him. They never told me to deal with it on my own or said that I had to stay with him.

"My parents loved me enough to stand up for me. I am glad they did. I am certain that if I had not told my parents about Ramon, I would either be dead or married to him and still enduring abuse."

After ending her relationship with Ramon, Alejandra met another young man, Henry, at a New Year's Eve party. "He was a great guy, nothing like Ramon," Alejandra wrote. Nevertheless, she was somewhat thrown by his respectful treatment. In her own words, Alejandra admitted that she had become "irresponsible" in her actions. Two months into the relationship, she became pregnant. While her parents were "devastated" when they heard the news, they remained supportive of her.

"My parents told me that they would support me in whatever decision I made. And they also reminded me that I did not have to stay with Henry, if I did not want to," Alejandra recalled.

Alejandra and Henry were married five months later. Their daughter was born that same year, and they now have another daughter. Henry and the two girls were all there to see Alejandra graduate from college with a B.A.

Despite the stalking, the emotional and physical abuse, and her becoming pregnant before being married, Alejandra's current situation suggests a hopeful future. However, what factors accounted for Alejandra's becoming involved and remaining in an abusive relationship in the first place? Moreover, why, after Ramon had yelled obscenities at her, pinched her, bruised her, bitten her, refused to use a condom during sex, and stalked her, did Alejandra continue to stay with him? Why, after months of emotional and physical abuse that her friends noticed and from which they tried to protect her, and after the confusion and despondency that led to a suicide attempt, would a teenage woman continue to date such an abusive partner? Was Alejandra's experience typical of other young women who could not separate from their abusive partners?

The survey data indicate that Alejandra is not alone in her confusion about what constitutes abusive behavior. Nor is she alone in being confused about how to respond to it. Rather, the data suggest that a substantial number of young teenage women have similarly experienced violent teen dating relationships. Like Alejandra, an even greater number are not sure about how to respond to situations when ostensibly violent behaviors occur.

What accounts for the fact that a substantial number of teenage women become involved in abusive or even violent dating relationships? Once involved, what makes it so difficult for them to end these relationships?

Why Teenage Women Become Involved

Before examining the whys and wherefores that lead teenage women into violent dating relationships, there are two caveats to propose. First, while both logic and statistical methodology make it possible to establish correlations between factors associated with teen dating violence, establishing causality between these factors is methodologically more problematic. Although one's involvement in a violent dating relationship may be related to factors such as one's socioeconomic background or psychological maturity, it is methodologically cavalier to conclude that a teen's involvement is *caused* by one of these factors. Thus, describing correlations among factors does not necessarily establish causality.

Second, much of what we postulate about why teens become involved and remain in violent dating relationships is derived from research conducted with adult women involved in abusive relationships. As discussed earlier, the experiences of teenage women somewhat parallel those of adult women in abusive relationships. However, there are some very important distinctions. As discussed in Chapter Three, adult women have greater access to legal redress and social services than teenage women. Further, they also have more life experience than their young teenage counterparts. Consequently, drawing conclusions about teens based on data from adult women may be inappropriate, inconclusive, or even misleading.

Aware of the caveats in establishing the causes of teen dating violence, and in generalizing from the experiences of adult women to minors, what factors can be linked, at least logically or statistically, with a young woman's involve-ment with an abusive partner? The literature on intimate partner abuse between adults and the data from my survey suggest at least four factors that may be related to a teen's becoming involved and remaining in a relationship with an abusive partner. These include a young woman's lack of self-esteem, her unrealistic expectations and pressures to conform, the experience of ob-serving violence in the home, and a lack of frames of reference against which to evaluate her experiences.

A LACK OF SELF-ESTEEM

In the popular culture, having a lack of self-esteem or a lack of regard for one-self seems to be the explanation for everything from being a school bully, to being a wallflower, or being either an abuser or a victim. Without self-esteem, psychologists and social workers conclude, people are unable to love them-selves. This results in a likeliness to judge themselves as being unworthy of the love of others. To compensate for the lack of love they feel, whether self-love or love of others, they sometimes go overboard and give themselves away in an effort to please others. They can be desperate to make themselves more lov-able. Thus, it is commonly held that a teenage woman might become involved in an abusive relationship because she lacks the self-esteem or self-love that makes her secure in herself. Even as she negotiates the give-and-take of trying to relate maturely with her partner, she may deny her own needs and turn her-self over totally to the one she is trying to please.

Further, teenage women without self-esteem may be more likely to become involved in codependent or addictive relationships than women whose self-esteem is stronger.[1] Specifically, a woman may try to gain some self-esteem by involving herself with a partner who makes her feel wanted or needed, even when that person is abusive and tries to convince her that she is worthless, ugly, will never find another boyfriend, and cannot make it on her own with-out him. Despite engaging with a partner who is jealous, intimidating, posses-sive, and controlling, or who is even physically or sexually abusive, a woman may nevertheless decide that this partner needs her, and so he becomes vital to her self-esteem.[2]

Pressure exerted by peers or parents, or societal expectations to find a male partner for her fulfillment as a woman may serve to reinforce a teen's low self-esteem. As Jaffe et al. (1992) note, the self-esteem of many teenage women is very much tied to their ability to get a boyfriend.[3] Consequently, many refuse to break up with abusive partners regardless of their behavior.[4] For example, when a young teenage woman who lacks self-esteem hears her boyfriend tell her that she is ugly, unlovable, or unable to function apart from him, she is especially vulnerable to accepting his opinions as true. Lacking other dating experiences, and without a strong self-image and comfort about who she is when she is dating, his comments may make sense to her. Rather than considering that his expectations are unrealistic or even unhealthy, she may falsely conclude that she has failed him, that she is bad, or that she is unworthy of respect. In the worst situations she may even deem herself at fault and, therefore, deserving of her boyfriend's emotional, physical, or sexual punishment. She will accept the blame the abuser shifts to her, regardless of who is at fault for the difficulty.

To what extent did the young women in the survey provide evidence of a lack of self-esteem? While far from a methodologically valid and reliable psychological test, several questions on the survey provided data about some indicators of self-esteem. For example, I asked the teens about the extent to which they felt confident about their abilities to make friends, to succeed academically, and to find boyfriends who would respect them.

Of the 499 young teenage women who responded to the survey, 57.5 percent agreed with the statement that they were good at making friends, and 31.1 percent strongly agreed. Thus, 86.6 percent expressed positive feelings about their abilities to make friends. Conversely, very few of those surveyed thought they were not good at making friends. Specifically, 2.4 percent either disagreed (1.8%) or strongly disagreed (.6%) that they were good at making friends. Nine percent (9%), however, neither agreed nor disagreed with the statement (6.2%) or said that they did not know if they were good at making friends (2.8%). Thus, over 11 percent of those surveyed expressed doubt about whether they were good at making friends.

Similarly, a high percentage of the respondents (83.8%) reported that they were proud of their academic abilities. As a group, however, they did not feel as strongly positive about their academic abilities as they did about their abilities to make good friends. For example, 27.9 percent strongly agreed with a statement that they were proud of their academic accomplishments, and 45.9 percent agreed. Slightly less than ten percent (9.8%) strongly disagreed (2.2%) or disagreed (7.6%) with the statement, while 16.4 percent neither agreed nor disagreed (15%) or said they did not know (1.4%) if they were or were not proud about their academic abilities.

Although the majority of respondents expressed confidence in their abilities to make friends or reported that they were proud of their academic accomplishments, substantially fewer reported strong positive feelings about their abilities to find a boyfriend who would respect them. Specifically, only 69.2 percent reported that they either agreed (39.5%) or strongly agreed (29.7%) that they were confident about their abilities to find a boyfriend who would respect them. Ten percent either disagreed (7%) or strongly disagreed (3%) with this statement; 13 percent reported that they neither agreed nor disagreed while 7.8 percent said they did not know how to respond to it. Thus, almost 30 percent of the sample responded that they doubted their abilities to find boyfriends who would respect them.

The responses of teenage women who generally thought they were good at making friends were positively and significantly correlated (.01 level) with each of the following:

- having pride in their academic abilities;
- feeling confident that they will find boyfriends who respect them;
- feeling good about how they relate to boys.

Confidence about finding a boyfriend who would respect them was also positively and significantly related to feeling good about the ways they relate to boys. Not unexpectedly, confidence in being good at making friends, pride in academic ability, believing they can find a boyfriend who will respect them, and feeling good about the ways they relate to boys were negatively correlated with their experiences of having been emotionally, physically, or sexually abused by a boyfriend. Basically, those young women who felt good about their abilities in these three areas were unlikely to experience abusive dating relationships.

Did the respondents who gave answers that demonstrated some feelings of inadequacy about academic or social skills give answers that correlated positively with their conclusions that they had been emotionally, physically, or sexually abused by a boyfriend? The answer to this question is "Yes": Decreasing confidence about academic abilities and social skills were positively correlated with more involvement in an emotionally, physically, or sexually abusive relationship. Thus, the greater the lack of confidence about academic abilities and social skills, the more likely a respondent was to report current or past involvement in an emotionally, physically, or sexually abusive relationship.

The majority of women who responded to the survey had positive feelings about their social and academic skills. However, a great proportion were more confident about their abilities to make friends or were more proud of their academic accomplishments than they were confident about their abilities to find boyfriends who would respect them.

While not a psychological measure of self-esteem, the responses to these questions nevertheless provide some indication of how young women in the sample regard themselves. The absence of positive feelings about their abilities to make friends, achieve academically, or meet boyfriends who will respect them correlates with tendencies to become involved in a violent dating relationship.

Because a lack of self-esteem is one factor that may make young women more susceptible to involvement in violent dating relationships than young women having higher levels of self-regard, social service providers and counselors should work to help young women improve their self-esteem. Since there are multiple causes of teen dating violence, however, they should not conclude that focusing solely on this factor would eradicate the problem. It can be dangerous to ignore other causes of teen dating violence because it may divert resources away from additional approaches that address other contributing factors. Furthermore, focusing on the problem of a lack of self-esteem focuses attention on a cause that may result in showering resources toward programs that help teenage women develop self-esteem at the expense of other programs sorely needed by these young women. While this is a noble effort, there is something insidious in this approach. Specifically, and once again, focusing on self-esteem as the problem erroneously makes young women the problem: Teen dating violence is caused by *their* lack of self-esteem and how *they* respond to male partners. More accurately, teen dating violence can be ascribed to controlling male partners who have not learned how to relate to their female partners without violence or abuse.

Teenage women, even those lacking self-esteem, should not have to expect abusive behaviors from their boyfriends. Whereas programs designed to help young teenage women gain, increase, or restore self-esteem are helpful, such programs should not divert attention from multidimensional programs, including those directed toward the role male partners play in abusive relationships.

UNREALISTIC EXPECTATIONS AND PRESSURES TO CONFORM

A woman's feelings of low self-esteem, self-worth, or self-love, when compounded by the verbal assaults of an abusive dating partner, are often reinforced in advertising and the media. Without a doubt, teenage women are bombarded with images that suggest what is "normal" in terms of physical appearance, dress, and behavior, especially behavior in relation to males. Regardless of one's age or life circumstances, teenage women receive media messages that tell them that society expects them not only to look and dress like Julia Roberts but also to conform their behaviors to the expectations of others. They must be especially careful in relationships with those to whom they want to be attractive and desirable. The alternative is clear: They will die "old maids" if they refuse to conform to their individual boyfriend's expectations. They will live unhappily if they question their boyfriends' behaviors—even those behaviors that more than hint of abuse. Lacking good parental modeling to counteract unrealistic life models and behavioral norms set forth by the media, it is not surprising that a number of young women accept the terms of dating relationships that are unhealthy or even deadly.

EXPERIENCES AT HOME

A third factor that predisposes some women to become involved in negative intimate partner relationships relates to their circumstances at home. For example, social scientists argue that growing up in a home where one sees violence between adults, or experiences violence at the hands of others in the home, are factors that predispose women to become involved and to remain in abusive relationships when they become adults.[5] Most often, the violence experienced was at the hands of an adult, whether a parent or a guardian (81%). In some cases, the violence occurred in the form of sexual abuse (almost 50%). However, another group of women who later became involved in intimate partner abuse as adults witnessed abuse and violence between adults (66%) where they "saw their mother or father being hit from 6 to 52 times (or more) a year."[6]

This evidence strongly suggests that women who were abused or who witnessed abuse as children may be more likely as adults to accept abusive behavior from an intimate partner. However, while such evidence exists regarding adult women, there is little, if any, corresponding research that documents whether teenage women in abusive relationships are also more likely to have experienced violence in the home than those who do not become involved in abusive situations. One can, therefore, only speculate about the causal nature of this relationship.

The reasons for this lack of research are again found in the difficulties researchers have in conducting research with minors. As discussed in Chapter Four, the compilation of such data, while highly desirable, is nevertheless very difficult to collect because of the problems associated with conducting research with minors whose parents must give consent before the research can begin.

If attempts to conduct research into this area continue to be resisted by Institutional Review Boards, whose concerns constrain a researcher's ability to ask questions about the home life of young teenage women, then there is little reason to expect that such research will be forthcoming. Unfortunately, exploring the vital links between a teen's home life and a predisposition to become involved in a violent dating relationship will not, more than likely, be investigated further.

Although there is strong evidence that seeing violence at home during one's childhood and living in poverty are factors that predispose women to become involved in abusive relationships later in life, the relationship between one's race or ethnicity and intimate partner abuse is unclear.[7] Contrary to what many believe, abusive relationships between intimate partners are no more or less characteristic of one ethnic, racial, or religious group than another. Teenage women, however, especially white teenage women, express the belief that becoming involved in an abusive relationship with a male partner is something that happens only to "others." In their minds, these others are usually people of color or members of racial or ethnic minorities or religious groups.

In discussing a book about teen dating violence as part of a teen dating violence prevention program, some of the students judged the book to be "wrong" because it described an abusive relationship that involved an Irish American teen who grew up in a middle-class neighborhood. Surely, they argued, her experience was atypical and more characteristic of teens in the "inner city." Translation: nonwhite and poor.

Although it is true that those who are poor tend to experience more violence in relationships than do those in economically prosperous families, domestic violence does not discriminate on the basis of race, ethnicity, or religion. Whereas more research is needed on this topic in terms of minors, there is no reason to believe that the same does not hold true for abusive relationships among teen dating partners. Thus, one would expect that lower-income white teenagers are as much at risk as lower-income minority teenage women because income seems to be the decisive factor, not race or ethnicity.

This fact is important for teachers, counselors, and social workers working to alert young teenage women to the signs of teen dating violence. Young women living in poverty or those who are members of racial, ethnic, or religious minorities, should know that they are not alone in their experiences with abusive dating partners. Teen dating violence is not just one more inevitable "pathology" associated with one's socioeconomic position or one's racial, ethnic, or religious heritage. Although in some cultures it might be argued that it is "acceptable" to beat women partners, domestic violence in the United States is a crime. Moreover, the state is obligated to protect a woman from an abusive partner, regardless of cultural "norms." To accept being beaten or abused because it is "typical" in one's culture not only does little for one's sense of personal efficacy but also ignores the fact that a crime has been committed.

By distinction, for white teenage women to persist in the belief that teen dating violence is something that probably could not happen to them is equally dangerous. In fact, without the understandings that modify their misguided perceptions of reality, white teenage women may be severely handicapped in recognizing the signs of abusive relationships once they become involved in them. For example, because they think that being involved in an abusive relationship is something that only happens to others, one incident of physical abuse that should signal danger is, instead, misinterpreted as an aberration because "only poor black and Hispanic girls" get involved in these types of relationships. They may also decide that "when he hit me, that wasn't dating violence. It was just a mistake. It won't happen again." Some young white

women believe themselves immune from the violence of an abusive dating relationship because they incorrectly stereotype violence among partners as
being more characteristic of racial or ethnic minorities where women seem
more subservient to men. Because of these misperceptions, they may be taken
more off-guard by their respective partners' behaviors than teenage women
living in minority communities.

A LACK OF EXPERIENCE AND FRAMES OF REFERENCE

Those new to dating relationships do not have enough experience to shape a
frame of reference against which to judge the "normalcy" of their relationships with intimate partners. Thus, teenage women may sometimes mistake
abuse for love because it is personal, it is passionate, and intense attention is
being paid to them. However, passion and attention may derive not from love
and concern but from their partners' anger or control over them.

As discussed in Chapters Five and Six, the survey data suggest that the majority of respondents seemed to have a good idea about what constitutes unacceptable behavior in a dating relationship. However, the data also suggest that
a substantial number are willing to tolerate violence or are ambivalent about
how to respond to a spectrum of abusive behaviors. It is particularly surprising
that the respondents are more ambivalent and confused about how to respond
to blatantly abusive behaviors. For example, although emotionally abusive behaviors would seem to be less violent, they were more confused about rejecting physically or sexually abusive behaviors.

What are some possible explanations for a young woman's having more
clarity about rejecting emotionally abusive behaviors than about rejecting
physically or sexually abusive behaviors? One hypothesis is that when a teen
experiences a behavior that is physically as opposed to emotionally painful,
she is more likely to rationalize the behavior: The physical pain he inflicted
was "accidental." He just got "carried away." It was "my" fault. For example,
having one's arm twisted while rough-housing is perceived as less abusive
than being "dissed" in front of one's friends. Because these actions are less
common, they may incorrectly construed as "playful" or accidental. In the
worst case, physical abuse may be viewed as justly deserved punishment.
Thus, a teenage woman may be more ambivalent about or willing to accept
patently physically abusive behaviors when she otherwise easily rejects emotionally disrespectful or controlling behaviors. Further, she may also feel less
fearful of expressing her feelings about verbal put-downs and other forms of
emotional abuse whereas saying "No" to physical assaults may result in more
of the same.

What might help teenage women better evaluate the behaviors they are experiencing? Whereas more positive dating experiences would certainly provide

a framework to help them assess whether what they are experiencing is a one-time accident or the beginning of a pattern of behavior, young women typically do not have the life experiences to form such a framework. Moreover, what they perceive as normal from the media, whether truly normal or not, is not necessarily healthy. They can see and evaluate the behavior of others, such as their parents or other adults, but how candid are their parents apt to be about their struggles with their partners? Even if the adults were forthcoming, to what extent are teens likely to believe that adult experiences are relevant to their own?

Teens can talk to their friends. However, their friends are also often bereft of dating experiences and behavioral frameworks. Moreover, though their peers might be eager to help, such "help" could result in the "blind leading the blind" scenarios.

Apart from personal experience or fruitful conversations with adults or others, teenage women will find it difficult to assess whether they are involved in healthy or unhealthy relationships. This is especially true when, in the absence of conversations with adults who have some experience in judging what is going on, the media and cultural or societal norms send out conflicting messages about what constitutes normal or healthy dating behaviors. Sadly, young teenage women do not often have the type and depth of information that will help them develop the instincts that direct them away from controlling and abusive male partners.

Without experience and frames of reference for evaluating their dating experiences, teenage women may find that education and information are their best aids in assessing what is happening to them in dating relationships. As will be discussed in Chapter Eight, parents are the first source of education and information. Lacking parental involvement, teenage women express some willingness to turn to a second source of assistance—educators or church-based personnel. Peers also are an important source of information or, as is more often the case, misinformation. Because those in trouble are most likely to turn to peers, it is also important to teach friends how to help friends by providing them with education and information and, perhaps, some training as peer counselors.

Why Teenage Women Stay Involved

In trying to understand the factors that predispose young women toward becoming involved in violent dating relationships, it must be noted that not every young woman characterized by either one or more of these factors necessarily becomes involved with an abusive partner. Indeed, the data show that many become involved in healthy dating relationships with male partners, even if they lack self-esteem and dating experience, or do not come from "model" homes. However, if they do become involved in an ostensibly violent dating relationship, then why do so many of them remain in such relationships?

Again drawing upon evidence from adult women in abusive relationships, research suggests that most women do not *want* to remain in abusive situations. While most adult women try to get away from their abusive partners, research shows that it takes as many as five to seven attempts to leave before they actually make the separation. Because "violence works to control the victim," it usually takes a long time for a victim to leave her abuser.[8] A study in Quincy, Massachusetts, for example, reports:

> 60% of the women who took out restraining orders reported 12 or more incidents of abuse in the prior year alone. Only 3% took legal action after the first episode. Police had already been to the home an average of five times before the victim sought the court's help and got a restraining order.[9]

Understandably, a woman living with her abuser can become isolated from others through the controlling actions of her partner. She is often unaware of or cannot access the types of social and legal resources that will assist her in leaving the abuser. Moreover, an abused woman who lives with her abuser may be kept financially dependent on him because he refuses to allow her to work outside the home. Thus, she has no means of making a living apart from him. Without money or transportation, it will be difficult for her to find alternative shelter, even among the shelters that exist to serve such women. Moreover, without education or training, or without health care or financial resources for herself and her children, she may be afraid to leave even the most abusive situation.

Abused women fear losing custody of their children if they separate from their abusive partners. The fear of losing their children is not unfounded. According to the Quincy Report, the Massachusetts Supreme Judicial Court found that "men win custody in 70% of the cases in which they fight for it. The reason for this may be that the batterer can afford an attorney while the victim cannot."[10]

Courts are not always sympathetic to the actions of a woman who is trying, sometimes clumsily, to separate from her abusive partner. Some in the court system have expressed frustration at the way women often seem to "toy" with police officers and the courts. For example, a woman will sometimes call the police when abuse is occurring, but then deny the abuse when police officers come to her assistance. In some cases, the abused woman, in defense of her abusive partner, will turn on the police officers. Such a response is frightening, even to seasoned veterans. Illustrating such fears, one officer told me that she would rather be chasing a suspect in an armed robbery than be called to a "domestic" where it was possible that either of the parties could turn on the officer.

Police officers are likely to feel ambivalent about how to respond to domestics, and they may also get frustrated when a woman drops charges once the complaint comes to court. Such frustration is understandable, especially as some police officers make Herculean efforts to support a woman's attempts to separate from her abuser. However, even as a woman tries to separate from an abuser, the violence between her and her partner is likely to escalate.

It is no wonder, therefore, that a woman is often ambivalent about dropping complaints in order to placate a partner whose capacity to inflict violence on her increases, even as she waits for a court appearance. For example, studies have found that the violence increases when a victim tries to leave her abusive partner. Further, women are in the greatest danger of being murdered when they try to leave.[11]

Thus, even women who are serious about trying to get away from their abusers often appear as though they are not. Such inconsistent behavior, however, should not be mistaken for an unwillingness to separate from the abuser so much as an action generated from pure fear. "Irrational" responses can become quite rational when women may fear retaliation from their abusers. Contrary to some beliefs, most adult women do want freedom from their abusers. In fact, through their access to and the coordinated efforts of social service agencies and the courts, many are able to escape from abusive partners. However, can the same be said of teenage women?

The reasons teens stay in abusive relationships, whether they make such efforts to separate from abusive partners, and the extent to which their reasons and efforts differ from adult women, are not well known. Clearly, the situation of a teenager living at home is different from that of an adult living with an abuser. While both adults and teens are not generally financially independent, teens typically lack the training and education that are necessary to obtain a job. Further, teens living at home are less likely to have a child that also needs protection.

Like many adult women, a teen may become isolated from her friends and be hesitant to talk to others, especially adults, about her predicament. Alejandra, for example, recalled that Ramon was "so controlling" that eventually, she "was all Ramon had." "He rarely associated with his friends and I rarely associated with mine," she remembered. "On occasion, I managed to spend a few minutes with my friends, only because I was fortunate to have them as classmates."

Apart from the controlling efforts of their boyfriends, what are some of the reasons that teenage women like Alejandra are so reluctant to seek help from others? What factors deter them from seeking help from those most interested in and responsible for protecting them?

Disincentives to Seeking Help

According to the survey data, many respondents reported that they would be very reluctant to tell their parents if they were to become involved in a physically violent dating relationship. In the sample, divided into those who had dated during the past year and those who had not, the "daters" were more hesitant to discuss their problems with their parents than were nondaters. Specifically, 76.8 percent of the daters said they would definitely or might tell their parents whereas 90.5 percent of the nondaters expressed such an opinion. Were the teenage women equally reluctant about discussing their troubles with others who might be involved in their lives, for example, relatives other than parents? School or church personnel? Or friends?

Generally, respondents were more willing to tell an older brother or sister about their involvement in a physically violent dating relationship than they were willing to tell their parents. Specifically, for daters, 88 percent would definitely or might talk to an older brother or sister about being involved in a violent dating relationship compared to 90.5 percent of the nondaters. Conversely, 8.9 percent and 6.4 percent of the daters and nondaters, respectively, said they would definitely not discuss this type of situation with an older brother or sister, assuming they had one.

Beyond the immediate family, however, a large percentage of both groups were reluctant to disclose any involvement in a physically violent dating relationship. For example, 26.1 percent of the daters said that they would definitely not tell a relative other than a parent or brother or sister, whereas 19.1 percent of the nondaters expressed the same opinion. Nevertheless, the majority of each group, 66.8 percent of the daters and 76.6 percent of the nondaters, said they would discuss their situation with a relative other than a parent or brother or sister.

Because institutional personnel are even further removed from the family than parents or siblings, one would expect that the young women in each sample would be even more reluctant to discuss their problems with someone from their school, their church, or their community. The data indicate that many, although not the majority, are indeed disinclined to speak to someone outside the family about problems in dating relationships.

For example, the data reveal that 42.7 percent of the survey respondents who dated during the past year said they definitely would not tell a teacher about their problems. Nondaters, however, though still disinclined, were more willing than daters to talk to a teacher. In comparison with daters, 25.5 percent said they definitely would not tell a teacher. One percent (1%) of the daters definitely would not talk with a teacher compared to 5.3 percent of the nondaters; and 47.6 percent of the daters might tell a teacher compared to 56.4 percent of the nondaters. In contrast to daters, nondaters expressed more confusion about what they would do: 12.8 percent of the nondaters said they did not know what they would do compared to 8.7 percent of those who had dated during the past year.

The respondents were, however, slightly more willing to talk with a school counselor than to a teacher. Compared to the one percent who definitely would tell a teacher, 15.9 percent of those who dated during the past year definitely would tell a school counselor. Compared to the 5.3 percent of the nondaters who definitely would tell a teacher, 20.2 percent would definitely tell a school counselor. By contrast, only 27.4 percent of the daters and 21.3 percent of the nondaters said they definitely would not talk to a counselor. The percentages of daters and nondaters who definitely would not talk to a teacher were 42.7 percent and 22.5 percent, respectively.

Somewhat surprisingly, survey respondents were less reluctant to discuss involvement in a physically abusive relationship with priests or clergy persons than they were with teachers. For example, 6.4 percent of the daters and 9.6 percent of the nondaters said they definitely would tell a priest or a clergy person about their involvement in a physically violent relationship. These numbers contrast with the one percent and 5.3 percent of the daters and nondaters, respectively, who said they would talk with a teacher. However, the data show that those who "might tell" a priest or clergy person (29.8 percent and 33 percent for daters and nondaters, respectively) are fewer than those who might tell a teacher (47.6 percent and 56.4 percent, respectively). Nevertheless, similar proportions of both daters and nondaters definitely would not confide in a priest or clergy person (49.2 and 38.3 percent, respectively) as definitely would not confide in a teacher (42.7 percent and 25.5 percent, respectively).

To tell or not to tell? Perhaps a young woman's ability and desire to share her "secret" with an adult may be tied to the degree to which she values the adult's positive image of her. Fearing that she may look "bad" in the adult's eyes may preclude her from being open with an elder. By contrast, a friend or peer might be easier to relate to because friends may be more accepting and less judgmental. Indeed, the survey data seem to bear this out.

Of all possible audiences for a teenage woman to confide in regarding a physically violent dating relationship, the overwhelming choice was friends. For both those who had dated in the past year and those who had not, 82.1 percent and 86.2 percent, respectively, definitely would tell a friend; an additional

15.1 percent and 10.6 percent of daters and nondaters, respectively, might tell a friend. Only one percent of those who dated during the past year and 3.2 percent of those who had not dated reported that they definitely would not tell a friend. Further, very few respondents queried about confiding in a friend indicated that they did not know what they would do. Under the "misery loves company" banner, it is not surprising that these young women felt more comfortable sharing with friends because they can more easily relate to those who could also be experiencing similar situations.

Given the level of trust that teenage women have in their friends and the mistrust they feel toward adults, it is not surprising that most would be more comfortable confiding in a friend about their involvement in a physically abusive relationship. The friend, whether a male or a female, may be able to lend an empathetic ear. However, as a peer, it is unlikely that even the best of friends is able to do much more than listen. Even as age and experience limit the perspective of the abused, they also limit the quality of advice most teenage friends are able to offer another. Even when their instincts and advice are sound, they may be limited in their capacities and resources to help their friends implement a strategy for disengaging from abusive partners.

Alejandra's friends, for example, recognized the danger of their friend's involvement with Ramon.

> *For months, my friends suspected something was going on, but they weren't quite sure what. Their suspicions were confirmed one day when they saw Ramon pinch me. Disgusted by his actions, they quickly intervened and walked with me to class.*

Nevertheless, Alejandra continued to see Ramon, even as she saw less and less of her friends.

> *On one occasion, I managed to spend a few minutes with my friends, only because I was fortunate to have them as classmates. They pleaded with me to leave Ramon, but I would not listen. 'I can't leave him. He needs me,' I would tell them.*

Alejandra stayed with Ramon, despite the good advice her friends had given her.

> *My classmates suggested that I apply for assistant editor of our school newspaper so that I wouldn't spend so much time with Ramon. When I told Ramon about my plans, he quickly questioned me: 'When are we supposed to spend time together?' Because of my obligation to Ramon and my lack of*

dedication to the newspaper, the position was given to someone else. Although I was disappointed, I acted nonchalant about it.

Alejandra was more committed to staying with Ramon, despite her friends' kind and thoughtful overtures to rescue her. Indeed, she had told her friends that she was in trouble. Although they were willing to help, they could not break the stranglehold Ramon had over Alejandra, and they could not break Alejandra's resolve to stay with Ramon.

> *It was during this time that I began to feel depressed and withdrawn from my family. Whenever Ramon was not there, I spent my afternoons locked in my bedroom (my parents always thought I was doing homework). I began to perfect my acting skills, altering my mood when I was with my family. However, as soon as I would return to my room, I would cry myself to sleep. Despite everything, my friends continued to be in contact with me every so often. Candy suggested that I get a job with her at a McDonald's downtown and I quickly agreed. Working at McDonald's was my chance to get away from Ramon. I had decided that things had to change, and I was going to start by changing myself. Although I was surrounded by new people at McDonald's, I was hesitant to make friends. I did not feel I could trust anyone. Candy made it a point to introduce me to everyone. She thought that if she could introduce me to someone new, I would leave Ramon.*

Her friends' plans to help her were apparently having some success. Alejandra would finally leave Ramon. However, as often happens in abusive relationships, the violence escalates when the abused tries to leave the abuser. It was then that Ramon began to harass her and stalk her, and nothing Alejandra or her friends did could stop him from becoming even more abusive.

> *Working at McDonald's gave me freedom, but Ramon was losing control of me and he didn't like it. Although I had ended our relationship, Ramon continued to pursue me as if nothing had changed. Things between us were getting out of hand, and I had had enough.*
>
> *One morning, at 7 a.m., the telephone rang. It was Ramon. I told him that I didn't want to talk to him and he said, 'If you don't talk to me, I'm going to keep calling you.' Afraid that my parents would wake up, I continued to talk to Ramon. I was due at work at 11 a.m. that morning, and Ramon refused to let me go. Then my father woke up to take me to work. I told my father that I was not scheduled to go to work that day. I was too embarrassed to walk in late so I decided that lying to my father was my only option.*
>
> *Because I was scheduled to work but failed to show up, a manager from*

*McDonald's telephoned my home and spoke to my father. My father was upset
with me and told me I was irresponsible. 'You cannot be doing these kinds of
things when you have a job, Alejandra,' he shouted.*

*I ran to my room feeling horrible. I decided this was it. I was tied to Ramon
and, because of him, my father was disappointed in me. Rather than face my
problems, I opted to die.*

It was then that Alejandra "swallowed every single pill" in a bottle of tranquilizers. Although her friends suspected that she had a problem, she did not
acknowledge to them how serious her situation was. Because she was embarrassed and had disappointed her father, she did not feel she could involve her
parents.

Embarrassment. Fear. Although Alejandra could hardly put words on these
feelings, the survey suggests that these are the key reasons why so many teenage women fail to inform others, especially adults, when they become involved
in abusive situations.

For many teenage women such as Alejandra, there is the fear that her parents would make her break up with her boyfriend, that they would "go ballistic," or that they would punish her for making a bad choice. However, when
she finally told her parents what was happening, none of these reactions occurred, at least not in the way Alejandra expected.

According to Alejandra, her mother "suspected that something was going
on." Her mother was right. There was a great deal going on. Alejandra and
Ramon were having sex, even when Alejandra "did not want to." Moreover,
Ramon refused to use a condom. Alejandra's main concern at this time, however, was not that she was being sexually abused or that the abuse was ongoing.
She did not equate Ramon's unwillingness to use a condom with sexual abuse.
Nor did she think that when Ramon forced her to have sex, she was being
raped. Rather, Alejandra's greatest worry was that she might get pregnant.
Given societal responses to pregnant unmarried women, it was no wonder
that Alejandra worried. In all likelihood, she would have been held solely responsible for the pregnancy. Moreover, she would probably have to face alone
the consequences of their joint behavior.

Alejandra's Mother "confronted" her.

*Although I was screaming for help on the inside, I denied every allegation
my mother made about Ramon. I told her that he loved me and that nothing
was going on.*

Alejandra was not about to tell her mother what was happening to her until
her desperation became so extreme that she tried to commit suicide. It was not

until after she swallowed "every single pill" in a bottle in her mother's medicine cabinet that Alejandra told her what had happened. Even then, however, her cry for help was not really to her mother but to Ramon whose attention, sympathy, and concern she wanted to attract.

> *Realizing what I had done, I ran to my mom and told her what happened. She ran to the washroom, grabbed the bottle, and threw me into the car. My mom cried all the way to the hospital. I felt horrible. I never intended to hurt my mom. All I wanted to do was make Ramon aware of what he was doing to me.*
>
> *Because I had swallowed so many pills, my stomach had to be pumped. My mom stood by me as the ER nurse inserted a tube all the way down my throat and into my stomach. Tears rolled down my mom's face as she quietly prayed for me. After the horrific procedure was over, I told my mom I was sorry. I never realized how my actions would affect my family until I saw them gather around me with tears in their eyes. Still, my only thought was 'Where's Ramon?' I wish he had been there to hear what the nurse had told me: 'Did you know that the pills you took are actually tranquilizers?' the nurse asked. I said, 'No, I didn't know.' 'Young lady, if you had waited a few more minutes before coming here, you would have died.'*

Alejandra was not concerned about dying. Although she was remorseful about the toll that her suicide attempt took on her parents, she was not yet willing to change. She simply wanted Ramon. Nevertheless, in spite of her myopia, Alejandra's parents did not "go ballistic." They did not punish her, and they did not force her to break up with Ramon. All of this was fine with Alejandra because, although she was being abused, she did not really want to break up with Ramon. So, she did not break up with him.

> *I wanted to tell Ramon. I wanted to gain his sympathy. I told him what happened. Because he was not there to see it, he did not believe me. I was exhausted and out of ideas. I continued to endure Ramon's behavior.*

Although there was so much more to Alejandra's story than she told her parents, she failed to confide in them. Why was Alejandra so unwilling to ask for help from her parents? For that matter, why are teens in similar situations united in refusing to share their pain with their parents?

Embarrassment. Isolation. Fear of retaliation or punishment. Lack of knowledge about where to get help. These are some of the reasons why Alejandra and many of the survey respondents were reluctant to tell their parents about being involved in a violent dating relationship.

EMBARRASSMENT

Less than half of those responding to the survey (34.3%) either strongly agreed (8.2%) or agreed (26.1%) that they would not tell anyone about being involved in a physically violent dating relationship because they would be embarrassed. An additional 15 percent neither agreed nor disagreed (10.8%), or responded "don't know" (4.2%). Over half of the respondents (50.7%) strongly disagreed (26.7%) or disagreed (24%) that they would be embarrassed to tell anyone about being involved in a physically violent dating relationship.

Were they the "embarrassed ones" because they thought their difficulty was personal and something they should handle by themselves? For 43.3 percent of the respondents, this seemed to be a concern. Although 56.7 percent of the respondents either strongly disagreed (29.4%) or disagreed (27.4%) that a reason not to tell anyone about being involved in a physically abusive dating relationship was because it was "something they should handle themselves," slightly over 18 percent (18.1%) neither agreed nor disagreed, agreed (15.3%), strongly agreed (5.4%), or responded "don't know."

Alissa's words illustrate the reluctance of many to involve their parents in their problems.

> *I didn't tell my mother because I didn't want to worry her. I was also fearful, that he would hurt my family if I did. And if I told my mother, I'd get lectured to death. So I didn't tell my parents. I could take care of myself and I didn't want to put them in harm's way. I didn't want to get them involved.*

Although they might be embarrassed, the young women in the sample were not as inclined to think that people would laugh at them or make fun of them if they were to reveal their involvements in violent dating relationships. Specifically, 84.7 percent either strongly disagreed (49.1%) or disagreed (35.6%) that they would not tell anyone because they feared being laughed at. Almost 6 percent (5.8%) neither agreed nor disagreed, 4.2 percent responded "don't know," and 5.2 percent strongly agreed (1.6%) or agreed (3.6%).

When asked about the degree of their concern that the people they told would make fun of them, their answers were similar. Specifically, 87.9 percent strongly disagreed (60.8%) or disagreed (27.1%) that this was a concern.

ISOLATION

If the teens told anyone, did they think those whom they told would believe them; and if they were believed, would anyone care enough to help? Rather than being helpful, would others say that the teens deserved what happened? Would it be futile to try to involve someone else in their problems? Were they really alone?

The data show that the majority of teenage women do not think it futile to involve someone in helping to solve their problems. Furthermore, they do not lack a sense of personal efficacy or believe that they would be bereft of support. Some women, however, may share Alissa's experience.

> *When I asked for help, my mother again insisted, 'You have to work this out yourselves.' She heard Dave say that he was going to kill me and she told us to handle it ourselves. So why would she help? It was one tangled ball. Even after the kids were born, Dave would take them out in the car when he was drunk. I couldn't find them. But my mother would never get involved, although she knew everything. She'd just say, 'You have to work out your own problems.'*

The survey data contrast Alissa's experience with the majority of teenage women who feel positively about being listened to and assisted. For example, when asked if they felt that those whom they told would not believe them, over three quarters of the sample (75.9%) either strongly disagreed (47.6%) or disagreed (28.3%) with the statement. By contrast, 2.8 percent strongly agreed; 8.6 percent agreed; 7.8 percent neither agreed nor disagreed; and 4.8 percent responded "don't know" to this concern.

As a slight variation on this question, I asked the respondents to consider whether others would believe them if they admitted their involvement in an abusive situation. Did they think that those whom they told would do anything to help them? In other words, to what extent did the respondents think others would be willing to assist them in their relational struggles?

The vast majority of the respondents (77.4%) did not believe that those whom they told and who believed them would be unwilling to help them. For 8.8 percent of the sample, however, the feelings were quite different. Specifically, 1.6 percent strongly agreed with the statement that those whom they told would be unwilling to help them, even if they believed them; 7.2 percent agreed with the statement, and 14.8 percent admitted they either had no opinion about the statement or did not know how to respond to it.

Six percent of the sample expressed opinions that reflected their belief in a total lack of efficacy. This group believed that, even if they told someone about their problems, their situations would not change in any way. Even apart from their beliefs about how their boyfriends might respond if they were to discover that their girlfriends had revealed their involvement in a physically violent relationship, the sense of victimization, isolation, and desperation must have been acute for these young women.

Although the support that Alejandra's parents gave her is what most of the survey respondents seem to expect, a small minority nevertheless feared that those they told would respond as did Alissa's mother. They feared their parents or others would say they just "deserved it" or that they would be told that it was "their problem" and something they should handle themselves.

Specifically, 67.9 percent strongly disagreed with not revealing their involvement in a violent dating relationship, believing that those whom they told would say they "deserved it." Another 21.7 percent expressed the same feeling, but with less intensity or conviction. For those who strongly agreed (2.2%) or agreed (1.6%) with the statement, or who were confused or had no opinion about how to respond to it (10%), the sense of futility and isolation would be, as it was for Alissa, truly overwhelming.

FEAR

What were they afraid of? What were the distasteful things that would happen to them or to their boyfriends if they were to tell others about being involved in a physically violent dating relationship?

Many in the sample seemed to be concerned that adults would force them to break up with their boyfriends. For example, 5.8 percent strongly agreed and an additional 12.7 percent agreed that the person(s) they told would make them break up with their boyfriends. By contrast, 65.7 percent either strongly disagreed (44.4%) or disagreed (21.3%) that such would be the result. Almost 15 percent (14.8%) expressed ambivalence about what they thought would happen. Thus, many of the young women in the sample feared that if they told anyone about their involvement in an abusive relationship, the persons whom they told would try to force them to break up with their boyfriends, even when they did not want a break-up to occur.

Alejandra's parents, however, did not force her to break up with Ramon. Perhaps they did not realize the gravity of her problem, either because she had not sufficiently clued them in on the details, or because they themselves may have been in denial about the seriousness of the problem. They did, however, voice their concerns and stood by her, especially in the emergency room after her suicide attempt. Despite her parents' concern, however, Alejandra still continued to chase Ramon, even as she insisted that she was trying to break up with him.

If a substantial number of the teenage women in the sample feared that someone would try to force them to break up with their boyfriends, did as many worry that they would get in trouble with their parents if they admitted they were involved in a physically violent dating relationship? The answer is "Yes." Many young women worried that they would get in trouble with their parents. Just over 32% of the sample (32.1%) indicated that they were concerned that they would get in trouble with their parents. Almost 68 percent (67.9%) strongly disagreed (42%) or disagreed (25.9%) that they feared telling someone because they were afraid they would get in trouble with their parents.

Alissa, for example, was not so much concerned that she would get in trouble with her parents as be "lectured to death." Even after her suicide attempt, Alejandra did not seem worried that she would get into trouble with her parents when she told them about Ramon's abusive behavior. Once she decided to tell her father, his response indeed was anger, but it was not directed at Alejandra:

> *I was fed up with Ramon. So I decided that the only way I was going to rid myself of him was to tell my dad. I was not sure what kind of reaction I would get from my father. I just needed him to save and protect me. I told my father everything I had endured in my one-year relationship with Ramon. My father was furious, not at me, but at Ramon.*

Alejandra's father was angry, not with Alejandra, but with Ramon and with his parents. This is an important distinction that many young women do not seem to make in their decisions about whether to talk to their parents. Indeed, their parents may get angry, but in their efforts to protect their children, their anger may be directed more toward the boyfriends than toward their daughters.

Alejandra's father's response was quick, strong, and supportive. He did not tell Alejandra that it was her problem, or that she "deserved it." Rather, her father asked Alejandra to call Ramon's mother to relate every detail of their turbulent relationship. Ramon's mother was sympathetic and apologetic.

> *'Ramon is just like his father,' she said. 'He witnessed a lot of the abuse I went through.' Then Alejandra passed the phone to her father. With a stern voice, he said, 'I don't want your son near my daughter. Ever!' He quickly hung up the telephone. 'It's going to be all right, Alejandra,' he told me.*

Nevertheless, Ramon called the next day.

> *Whenever my parents would answer, he would hang up (I was ordered not to answer the telephone). My father was determined to take care of this. He had the call traced. The location was a pay phone near Ramon's aunt's home. My parents quickly got into the car and headed over there. When they returned home, I secretly asked my mom what had happened. My father attempted to speak to Ramon and his mother, but was asked to leave by Ramon's aunt. Before leaving, my father shouted, 'If you ever come near my daughter again, I am going to get a restraining order against you.'*

Like Alejandra's friends, Alejandra's father wanted to help. In contrast to Alejandra's friends, however, her father had leverage with Ramon's parents.

Moreover, Alejandra's father was aware of the legal redress available to Alejandra through the courts, and he was willing to use it.

Now that Ramon had been "put on notice" by Alejandra's father what, if any, did Alejandra think the implications would be for her and for Ramon? For example, was she worried that her father would take revenge on Ramon?

> *Ramon's aunt came out of the house and began a shouting match with my father. She began to blame me and say that I should leave Ramon alone. My mother decided to pull my father into the car before things got more out of hand.*

Were the survey respondents concerned that, if they told someone about being involved in a violent dating relationship, things could get "out of hand"? Alternatively, did they fear that those whom they told would seek revenge against their boyfriends? Conversely, did they worry that their boyfriends would seek revenge on them when they discovered that their private behaviors had been made public to adults?

Almost a third of the sample was concerned that the person(s)whom they told would take revenge on their boyfriends. Specifically, 10.3 percent strongly agreed and 22.2 percent agreed that the persons they told would try to hurt or take revenge on their boyfriends. Almost 25 percent (22.4%) of the sample was uncertain about whether such revenge would take place. Only 45.2 percent of the sample was fairly certain that revenge against their boyfriends would not result if they disclosed their involvement in a violent dating relationship. Specifically, 18.8 percent strongly disagreed and 26.4 percent disagreed that revenge would be the result.

Were the survey respondents worried that if they told someone about being involved in a violent dating relationship, their abusive dating partners would break up with them? The answer for the majority of respondents was "No," they did not seem to be concerned that their boyfriends would find out and break up with them. Specifically, 50.4 percent strongly disagreed and 23.7 percent disagreed that not telling anyone about their involvement in a violent dating relationship was influenced by a concern that their boyfriends would find out and break up with them. Only 8.4 percent either strongly agreed (2%) or agreed (6.4%) that such was a concern. However, 17.6 percent were unsure about how to respond to the statement.

Did many of the respondents fear that their boyfriends would find out and try to hurt them if they disclosed involvement in a violent dating relationship? Less than half of the sample (42.7%) either strongly disagreed (24.7%) or disagreed (17.9%) that a reason for not telling anyone about their involvement in a violent dating relationship was the fear that their boyfriends would find out and try to hurt them. Slightly over a quarter of the sample (25.6%) agreed that such a response was likely and 6.6% strongly agreed. Once again, the percentage of respondents who were not clear about how they thought their boyfriends would respond, either because they responded "neither agree nor disagree" (12.7%) or "don't know" (12.5%), was surprisingly large.

LACK OF KNOWLEDGE

According to the survey data, the vast majority of respondents believed they would know the signs of a violent dating relationship were they to become involved in one. In fact, 83.9 percent either strongly agreed (34.8%) or agreed (49.1%) that they would recognize the signs of a dangerous dating relationship. Only 2.6 percent strongly disagreed (.8%) or disagreed (1.8%) with the statement. A substantially higher percentage (13.6%), however, said they neither agreed nor disagreed with the statement.

These responses, however, need to be weighed against other questions in the survey. For example, respondents would not leave a boyfriend who forced them to have sex against their wills, suggesting that many respondents did not know that what they had experienced constituted both dating violence and rape. Further, although 20.3 percent of the respondents reported that a boyfriend had emotionally abused them, only 7.9 percent of the respondents reported that they had been involved in a violent dating relationship at one time or another. Obviously, many of the respondents did not consider emotional abuse to be the same as being involved in a violent dating relationship. The incongruity in these responses suggests that many of the survey respondents lack knowledge about the types of behaviors that are elements in a violent dating relationship.

Despite lacking good information about what is appropriate or inappropriate behavior in a dating relationship, over three-quarters of the sample (75.5%) believed they have the personal skills to get out of a violent relationship were they to become involved in one. Approximately three percent of the sample was clear that they did not have the personal skills to get out of a violent dating relationship. Illustrating a startling lack of self-assurance was the fact that 20.2 percent of the sample simply did not know whether they had the personal skills to leave a violent dating relationship, that is, over one-fifth of the respondents reported that they neither agreed nor disagreed with the statement.

Did the survey respondents think they had the knowledge about where to go for help if their boyfriends threatened them? Only 9.8 percent of the sample strongly disagreed (3%) or disagreed (6.8%) with the statement that they knew a place where they could go to get help if their boyfriends threatened them. Over one quarter (25.5%), however, reported that they neither agreed nor disagreed (5.2%) with the statement or said they did not know (20%) of a place to go; 64.9 percent either strongly agreed (12.3%) or agreed (43.6%) with the statement.

The responses to a similar query were somewhat different in terms of the numbers of participants who were unsure of how to answer the question. For example, when asked their opinions about whether they knew where to go for help to get out of a violent dating relationship were they to become involved in one, 9.4 percent strongly disagreed (1.5%) or disagreed (7.9%). These numbers are very similar to the 9.8 percent of the sample that responded similarly when asked if they knew a place where they could go if their boyfriend threatened them. However, 17.6 percent neither agreed nor disagreed with the more generic statement while over 25 percent responded with confusion to the more specific situation about a threatening boyfriend. Moreover, they were less secure about knowing a place to go for help in getting away from a threatening boyfriend when the situation was posed generically (72.9%) than they were when the question was phrased more specifically (64.7%).

Did the young teenage women in the sample really need to know about such resources, whether personal or institutional? Regardless of whether or not they have reported experiencing emotional, physical, or sexual abuse, how many of them thought they had *actually been* emotionally, physically, or sexually abused by their boyfriends?

The survey data suggest that the vast majority of respondents thought they had never been sexually (95.6%), physically (94.8%) or emotionally (79.7%) abused by a boyfriend. Moreover, the data indicate that far fewer reported being sexually or physically abused than reported incurring emotional abuse. However, the discrepancy between those who said they had been emotionally abused (20.3%) and those who had experienced being involved in a violent dating relationship (7.9%) suggests that many of the young women do not think emotional abuse is violent. At the time the survey was administered, 1.3 percent or six women in the sample believed they were currently involved in a violent dating relationship, and 95.6 percent said they were not. Slightly over three percent (3.1%) or 14 young women, however, were unsure about whether they were currently involved in a violent dating relationship. The uncertainty for these 14 women again suggests a lack of information and knowledge about what constitutes a violent dating relationship.

Stories related by teenage women clearly illustrate the uncertainties and the dilemmas they confront in trying to separate from abusive boyfriends. Even as they develop their own identities, grow to adulthood, and define their role within their families and among their friends, their involvement in social relationships with the opposite sex is yet one more venue where they can test role expectations, develop interpersonal skills, and differentiate between being liked, loved, or controlled by another.

Obviously, these years are trying for all teens and for those who are concerned about them, but this "growing season" can also be psychologically, physically, or sexually dangerous for a small but significant number of young women. Why do these teenage women become involved in relationships that are not only unhealthy but also violent, or even deadly, when others seem to avoid involvement in questionable or harmful relationships?

While it is true that a lack of self-esteem can undermine a young teenage woman's confidence and make her more susceptible to a relationship with controlling and abusive males, a lack of self-esteem cannot be the only factor that pushes some young women into the arms of abuse. The fact is that most teenage women are only beginning to build self-esteem during their adolescent years. Nevertheless, the vast majority is able to avoid involvement in abusive relationships. Additionally, they become involved in healthy, if sometimes turbulent, relationships with male partners that then help them make good choices about life partners, even if a relationship sours and a divorce occurs.

Research, especially in social learning theory, suggests that when adolescents experience violence in the home, whether between parents, among other adults, or personally, they may model the same dysfunctional behavior in their own interpersonal relationships that they saw in their own homes.[12] These experiences foster confusion about the difference between love and the violence that often accompanies jealous and possessive dating relationships.

The evidence, however, supports a stronger positive correlation between aggression in a male and his experience of violence in the home than the correlation between a woman's experience of violence at home and her level of aggression.[13] It is, therefore, less clear that a teenage woman will necessarily become abusive if she witnesses or experiences violence in her home. Moreover, it is not clear whether she will more readily accept the abuse of a male in later life. Even if we had data about the early experiences of teenage women and their later behaviors as adults, we still could not predict how "types" of young women may relate to their male dating partners. The lack of data to research these issues begs for additional research.

Finally, why do some young teenage women, although not the majority, yield to the controlling and unrealistic expectations of their boyfriends? Why are some young women, despite their lack of experience in social or dating situations, able to avoid the tragedy of abusive relationships with male partners?

The data suggest that while the pressures and effects of a patriarchal society may be difficult for many young women to escape, most do work through developmental issues without succumbing to the overtures of those who would control, possess, and abuse them. Even as young women are learning to frame their experiences, many seem to avoid becoming involved in abusive relationships.

Obviously, then, it is a combination of factors that interacts and that militates toward an adolescent's becoming involved in a violent dating relationship. Thus, while it is helpful to focus programs and resources on one or another of these factors, a comprehensive programmatic approach is needed to help adults identify and assist the young women who are most at risk for involvement in violent dating relationships.

In developing this approach, adults who serve, counsel, and develop programs for teenage women also need to understand why, once involved in abusive relationships, teenage women stay with their abusers and are reluctant to access resources, whether personal or institutional, that can help them separate from abusive partners. As the data and the stories of young women suggest, many are confused about what constitutes love or violence. They are also embarrassed to admit their involvement in an abusive relationship to anyone but their friends who, while being willing to listen and help, do not usually have the experience or the resources to be truly helpful. Also, fear prevents many from discussing their situations with adults. Will the adults respond with anger toward the abuser that will get out of control? Will they respond with anger toward the abused young woman and punish her, perhaps by making her break up with her boyfriend who, despite his behaviors, she believes still loves her? If he were to find out, will the abusive male retaliate with escalating abuse toward his partner, her friends, or her family?

The answers to these questions, especially for young teenage women, are unknown. What is known, however, is that many young teenage women, regardless of whether or not they had dated recently or in the past, are fearful. Their fear of such reactions provides them with good excuses to keep their own counsel if they become involved in a violent dating relationship. The teens, however, are not totally opposed to seeking the counsel of adults. Rather, the data suggest that the majority of teens were not afraid to confide in adults for fear that they would not be listened to. Instead, the vast majority were confident that they would be taken seriously and, having sought help, that their situations would change. All of this suggests that, although there are many reasons that teenage women stay involved in abusive relationships, most believe that help is available if they were to seek it out. They may not always know where to go for such help, but there is some willingness to seek help from family members as well as school and church personnel. If they can overcome their embarrassment, their isolation, and their fear, and if they can learn to view school and church personnel as trustworthy and helpful resources, teenage women involved in abusive relationships may be more forthcoming in seeking help about their dating problems.

CHAPTER 8

(NOT THE) CONCLUSION:
JUST THE BEGINNING

"He is his father. He drinks too much. He lied to me when he said he was going to school, and I found out that lying had become a habit with him. He promises to do things and he never comes through. He is very angry. He has taken on all his father's mannerisms—lack of respect for me, drinking, lying. Everything he didn't like in his father, he is."

The young man who used to take on his father in order to protect his mother, the young boy who had wished his father would leave, was now exhibiting many of the signs that Alissa saw in her abusive husband. For Alissa, a violent teen dating relationship had turned into a violent marital relationship. In addition, the violence her husband inflicted on her and her children is now being repeated a generation later in the uncontrolled anger of her sons.

Teen Dating Violence: A Real Problem

Is teen dating violence a problem? Alissa's answer would surely be "Yes," and a problem not only for the abused but also for those who witness the abuse. How much of a problem is it? Estimates about how many teenage women experience emotional, physical, or sexual abuse vary. This research suggests that, although the majority of teens do not experience teen dating violence, a substantial number do. In particular, large numbers of teens report experiences of various forms of emotional abuse. Further, the heart-wrenching stories shared by Alissa, Alejandra, and Maggie indicate that such violence not only exists but also that it can be physically brutal, sexually abusive, and sometimes lethal.

CONFUSION ABOUT WHAT CONSTITUTES ABUSE

Despite the violence in abusive relationships, many young women are never-theless confused about what constitutes physical or sexual abuse. In their con-fusion, they are reluctant to name it as such or to see it as part of an ongoing problem. To some degree, the same reluctance to name abusive behavior as an ongoing problem rather than as an isolated incident is also true for adults. Thus, in its causes, characteristics, and cycles, teen dating violence mirrors abuse in intimate partner relationships between adults. For both teenage and adult women, intimate partner violence includes a range of behaviors that can be categorized as emotionally, physically, or sexually abusive. Moreover, the cycle of violence that adult women experience and the profile of an abusive male characterize abuse in teen dating relationships.

To better define the specific profile of a *young* abusive male minor would be helpful. However, little research in this area has been undertaken. Without the benefit of such research, we are forced to rely on research conducted on or with adult male abusers. For adult male abusers, the issue seems to be the need to exert power and control over others, especially women. Lacking research on young abusive males, we can only assume that their issues are similar.

NOT QUITE THE SAME AS DOMESTIC VIOLENCE

Despite similarities to abusive domestic relationships between adults, teen dating violence differs from domestic violence in five significant ways.

Not Puppy Love. First, adults are more inclined to dismiss reported violence among teen daters as "puppy love." This does not usually happen to adult women who complain of domestic abuse. Adults who hold such attitudes or lack information about teen dating violence can too lightly disregard what teens tell them. Feeling "blown off," teenagers can then become reluctant to talk to adults about their relational problems.

No Easy Access to Courts. Lacking the involvement of parents or other con-cerned adults, teenage women cannot easily gain redress from the legal system. For example, obtaining orders of protection can often, although not always, be obtained only with the involvement of a parent or an adult. Thus, the second factor that differentiates teen dating violence from domestic vio-lence is access to the legal system. Minors will find it much more difficult to engage the attention of the court to obtain orders of protection without adult involvement, whether by parents, police officers, or states attorneys. Addi-tionally, they will find that the court's method for determining jurisdiction for their cases will be intimidating, complex, and confusing. Further, besides being leery about the ways that police officers and the courts will treat them, teens will sometimes find the legal maneuvering time-consuming and costly. By the time the courts get around to helping them, teens sometimes complain, the abuser has found out about their revelations. When this happens, the abuser is likely to become more threatening and more violent before the courts take any action.

No Easy Access to Social Services. Third, teenage women do not have access to the same array of social support services that are available to adult women. For example, because of building regulations, zoning codes, and licensure requirements, a minor cannot usually take refuge from an abusive boyfriend in a shelter for abused *women.* Nor, when trying to escape from an abusive boyfriend, can she be absent from school without parental knowledge and without being considered truant. Further, depending on the nature of her disclosures to school counselors, a teenage woman is usually limited in the number of times she can be seen in a counseling relationship before the counselor is obligated to inform the parents. For the counseling to continue, the parents must subsequently give consent. Thus, the minor's ability to act on her own and to avail herself of social and mental health services is sorely limited.

More Psychologically Damaging. Fourth, the psychological effects of abuse can be more debilitating and longer lasting for a teen because she is in a very vulnerable stage of emotional development. Because of her involvement in a violent dating relationship, teenage women in abusive relationships may, for example, have trouble developing self-esteem. They may adopt unhealthy eating patterns or have difficulty in finding and establishing healthy relationships with future dating partners. Silverman et al. (2001) found:

> The experience of physical dating violence (without reported sexual violence) was associated with substance abuse (heavy smoking, binge drinking, driving after drinking, cocaine use), unhealthy weight control (diet pill use, laxative use), sexual risk behavior (first intercourse before the age of 15 years, not using a condom at last intercourse, greater than or equal to 3 sex partners in the past three months), pregnancy, and suicidality (considered suicide, attempted suicide) among female adolescents.[1]

Sexual abuse was also associated with several of these factors.

As Silverman et al. (2001) note, teenage women engaging in such behaviors are more vulnerable to contracting sexually transmitted diseases than teens who are not abused by dating partners. Moreover, "suicide ideation and actual suicide attempts were approximately 6 to 9 times as common among adolescent girls who reported having been sexually and physically hurt by dating partners."[2]

Generational Carry-Over. Fifth, sometimes the violence that women experience as teens carries over into abusive marital relationships, either with the same or different partners. In these situations, "children who experience or witness violence in all three places (home, school, and community) are at highest risk for developing aggressive acting-out behaviors."[3]

Alissa's story illustrates that, even when the abusive relationship ends with abusers and victims separating from each other, the violence and anger of those who witnessed it can sometimes be transmitted to the next generation. Alissa shares her concerns about her sons.

> *Kevin has had the same girlfriend for years and is very caring of her. But he yells and screams at me in front of her. I am afraid that once I am not there to absorb his anger, he will take it out on another. I am afraid because he has very little control over his anger and tries to be the 'toughest,' like his dad. The thought of Kevin and Ron (the younger brother), carrying on this rage into their marriages and instilling it in their children would be more than I could bear. I think that would be the worst pain of all.*

Alternatively, Alejandra and Maggie seem to have been successful in developing healthy relationships with male partners who are not abusive. However, while Alissa has separated from her abusive husband, she is now a single parent trying to raise two teenage sons. The dating and domestic abuse she suffered is over, but the effects linger. Both of her sons, especially her older son, now exhibit some of the characteristics of an abusive personality. Sadly, when Alissa looks into the faces of her sons, she often sees her former husband's anger in her children's. The invisible peril has now imperiled another generation.

> *I had hoped that I had enough time with my 17-year-old before it was too late. Unfortunately, the damage was done.*

In the behavior of her sons, Alissa is now experiencing what many domestic violence counselors say is predictable: "Whether or not children are physically abused, they often suffer emotional and psychological trauma from living in homes where their fathers abuse their mothers."[4] For example, "Most experts believe that children who are raised in abusive homes learn that violence is an effective way to resolve conflicts and problems. Further, boys who witness their mother's abuse are more likely to batter their female partners as adults than boys raised in nonviolent homes."[5]

> *By now I knew that violence, whether physical or verbal, had become a way of life for me and my sons. I had hoped that once Dave left, we would work it*

out. Not that easy. We are all caught up in the pattern. I knew instinct made us all lash out verbally to protect ourselves. The boys were beginning to exhibit physical signs of anger—punching walls and throwing items. The verbal abuse was pointed at me, not because they were angry at me, but just because I was there. I wasn't going anywhere and they knew it.

The effects of intimate partner violence are real. They are significant, and they can choke off a happy future of those who have observed or experienced it. For teenage women, the effects may be especially toxic, negatively affecting their self-esteem, destroying self-confidence, eroding feelings of competence, and paralyzing their abilities to move into futures of healthy relationships.

Alissa, now trying to recover her life, is doing all she can to repair the damage.

I went into counseling through a domestic violence center. They helped me to cope with my immediate concerns regarding my doubts, if you can believe it, that I had about separating from Dave. Then there were the money concerns. Mostly, I needed to break the cycle.

How Much of a Problem?

To what extent is teen dating violence *really* a problem? Through their poignant stories, the pain and violence that Alejandra, Alissa, and Maggie experienced become palpable. Their experiences, however, have been shared by a number of teenage women. Specifically, as many as 22.2 percent of the survey respondents who dated within a year of the survey's administration indicated that they had experienced some form of emotional abuse; 5.7 percent reported they had been physically abused; and 5.4 percent reported that they had been sexually abused. Some young women have even suffered the same fate as Lisa Santoro: murdered by an ex-boyfriend who could not cope with the fact that his former girlfriend had decided to date another young man.

Although the majority of teenage women had not experienced violence in their dating relationships, a substantial number had experienced being beaten, stalked, raped, or murdered. In fact, compared to the 1.5 million women who are physically abused by partners each year, and the 25 percent of all women who will experience some form of physical and/or sexual abuse during their lifetimes, approximately 25 percent of adolescents will be similarly traumatized.[6] Thus, teenage women reported almost as much violence in their dating relationships as adult women. In view of such evidence, it is difficult to keep thinking that only adults become involved in abusive relationships.

Despite its prevalence among teens and the serious consequences that it has for their future dating and marital relationships, teen dating violence remains a relatively invisible peril. Parents seem especially unaware of the potential for violence in teen dating relationships. Reflecting on their own experiences as teens, they incorrectly assume that the violence in dating relationships is an adult problem and not something faced by teenagers or children. Though misguided, such thinking should not be unexpected insofar as most parents did not begin dating as early as teens today, typically at the age of 13.[7] However, when apprised of a potential or actual abusive situation involving their daughters, many nevertheless dismiss or downplay the seriousness of the problem. In so doing, these adults unwittingly undermine opportunities for the types of communication that will help them understand what their daughters are experiencing so that they can help them separate from their abusers.

Some Willingness to Seek Help

Despite their lack of awareness or limited preparation for dealing with such situations, and in view of the many real or perceived fears their daughters have about discussing problems with adults, parents and other family members remain key contacts for teenage women. The survey data indicate that the vast majority of teenage women felt some inclination to talk to parents or other relatives about their dating problems. They were, however, even more inclined to seek help from friends. In addition to parents and friends, teens also identified educators, church-based personnel, and the law enforcement community as being potential sources of help. Each of these groups has an important role to play in addressing the problem of teen dating violence. Even the scholarly research community can contribute to the amelioration of the problem.

ROLES FOR PARENTS

How might parents, guardians, and family members respond to the psychological and emotional complexities that confuse and undermine the self-esteem of those involved in abusive relationships? Family members should be the "front line" for information about the existence of teen dating violence, and they should engage in conversations with teenagers about how to avoid it. Specifically, what can they say or do that will be helpful?

First, they can acknowledge the existence of the problem, discuss it with other adults and friends, and initiate conversations with their children about it, preferably before dating begins. Despite what many adults think, the survey data suggest that teenage women are willing, although somewhat reluctant, to talk to adults about problems they are experiencing in dating relationships. Parents should learn the reasons for such reluctance and avoid berating or grounding their daughters if they become involved with partners who exhibit violence.

Second, if a teenage daughter suggests or complains about her boyfriend's behavior, then they should take her complaints seriously. They should not dismiss them as "puppy love," "growing pains," or "typical" emotional problems that teenagers encounter. Conversations with the male dating partner's family may be in order or, in extreme cases, the teen's parents may need to seek an order of protection. In seeking such an order, however, parents should work with school officials to understand whether and how their daughter will be protected from an abuser if he is a classmate.

Third, if contacted by school counselors, parents should focus less on any personal embarrassment they feel and more on their daughter's needs. Although there are exceptions, most school counselors do not call parents about problems such as teen dating violence unless they think the problem is severe and the health or well-being of a young woman is in danger. A call from a school principal or counselor should not be thought of as meddling but as the well-intentioned warning of a professional who usually has the best interests of the student at heart. At the very least, a follow-up meeting should ensue.

Fourth, attentive observation of a teenage woman's behavior can also reveal signs that she is in an abusive relationship. For example, consider whether a once-social young woman suddenly become withdrawn. Does she spend far less time with her friends and family than she did before she began dating her current partner? Does she always go out on dates alone with her boyfriend? Does she spurn opportunities to go out with her girlfriends, or in mixed groups of friends? While it is certainly normal for a teenager to want to spend time alone with her boyfriend, she is not generally well served by avoiding all social situations with her friends and family. Rather, such behavior *may* suggest that she is not so much "in love" as being controlled by a jealous boyfriend who resents it when "his girl" demonstrates that she can have a life apart from him. Asking her the right questions in a nonaccusatory fashion, and listening carefully as she shares what is going on in her life can help parents determine the true nature of her dating relationship.

Fifth, parents and their children can agree on a code word or expression that enables a young teenage woman to signal her parents that she is in trouble without being embarrassed or alerting an abusive boyfriend. The parents can then advise their daughters about what to do or, if necessary, personally come to their aid.

ROLES FOR FRIENDS

While parents play the primary role in helping young women to understand what it means to be respected emotionally, physically, and sexually, the survey data reveal that a teenage woman involved in a problematic dating relationship is most likely to lean on peers as her primary resource. Peers may lend sympathy and understanding. However, they seldom have access to the wisdom, life experience, or the resources that will help a friend separate from an abusive dating partner. For this reason, dating violence prevention efforts need to inform teenagers not only about how to avoid abusive relationships but also about how to help a friend in an abusive situation. Here, I quote the good advice provided by the Dating Violence Prevention Project of the Battered Women's Shelter in San Antonio, Texas.[8]

- Don't be judgmental. Never blame your friend for the abuse. It's *not* his/her fault.
- Help him/her find supportive adults.
- Help him/her make and carry out safety plans.
- Be there for him/her and listen to his/her concerns.
- Keep supporting him/her even after he/she breaks up with the abuser.
- Don't neglect your own life. Support yourself as well as your friend.
- Allow your friend to make the decision, even if it means he/she is not ready to leave the abusive relationship. Explain that it's not his/her fault. Understand that he/she needs to make the decision.[9]

In general, this advice suggests two things that friends can do to be supportive. First, provide a sympathetic and nonjudgmental response. Second, encourage the teen to seek the help of an adult.

There are a number of institutional supports available to teens to augment family support. In cases where parents are unwilling or unable to advise their children about the perils of this hidden violence, other adults can become the primary support for the imperiled teen. Who and what might their roles be?

ROLES FOR EDUCATORS

Although educators are aware of the problem of teen dating violence to varying degrees, most admit they have few ideas about how to prevent it or how to deal with it. Some schools have adopted teen dating violence prevention programs. These programs, however, vary widely in focus and duration. For example, some schools rely on a one-time presentation by a speaker such as a domestic violence counselor, a police officer, or someone with direct experience of teen dating violence. These may include survivors of abuse or people such as Tom Santoro and others who have "been there." In other cases, schools take a team approach. Here, counselors, teachers, police officers, domestic violence counselors, and survivors of abuse conduct workshops that extend from one to several days.

In more comprehensive programs, teachers, counselors, and school administrators work together and invite outside resources to join them in the implementation and design of dating violence curriculum intervention projects. These programs, often held over a period of a week or more, invite students to discuss the problem of teen dating violence in a workshop or classroom setting where movies and novels can be used to depict different aspects of the problem. In the hands of a creative teacher, for example, students might role-play or discuss the experiences of others depicted in novels such as Clarke's *The Breakable Vow*.[10] These experiences and books can offer opportunities for students to discuss "hypothetical" situations without necessarily revealing their personal experiences. In leading students through the material, educators assume two important roles: They are agents of accessibility and agents of information. As agents of accessibility and agents of information, what can educators do to assist their students who become involved in violent dating relationships?

First, educators need to make themselves accessible to teens before and after school. Although many high school students are not as able to "hang around" before and after school as they once did, and with other opportunities and responsibilities limiting their abilities to participate in extracurricular activities, those who do hang around will sometimes find adults in short supply. Like their students, teachers also have increased demands on their time that make hanging around outside of class time more difficult, if not impossible. However, for those teachers whose schedules allow them opportunities to meet and converse with students outside of class time, they may be surprised to learn that teens are inclined to talk with them about problematic dating relationships. When teens do approach their teachers or counselors, however, they need to feel safe. They need to feel heard. They do not need to feel judged or unaccepted. As most educators know, teens can sometimes respond negatively to a teacher's best intentions. Sometimes, for example, being asked a question can be construed as prying or being judged. Despite these risks and potential misunderstandings, educators should not be put off in their efforts to help teens work through relational dilemmas. Neither should they be discouraged from seeking opportunities, few as they may be, from "hanging around" after school because the data suggest that teens may be sufficiently interested in their advice to seek them out.

Second, educators need to know about the scope of teen dating violence. What behaviors describe teen dating violence and distinguish it from abusive relationships between adults? What is the difference between being teased or demeaned? When do roughhousing and wrestling become disrespectful or violent? What are the physical and circumstantial characteristics of rape? In other words, what does a teenage woman need to know to determine whether she has experienced abusive behavior and is involved in an abusive relationship? What does she need to know to learn that she needs help?

Third, educators need to be as creative in teaching their students about teen dating violence as they are about teaching their disciplines. For example, teachers can lecture in detail about the short and long-term consequences of abusive acts and how they harm both the abused and the abuser. There are other teaching strategies they can adopt, however. Some teachers have used hypothetical scenarios or case studies to help young men and women imagine and discuss the implications of remaining in an abusive relationship. Others have used role-playing, movies, novels, pamphlets, presentations from outsiders, dramas, diaries, and short stories to depict real or fictional stories about those involved in various aspects of teen dating violence.[11]

Fourth, while learning to recognize the signs of abusive relationships among their students, educators also need to help teens identify the characteristics of healthy interpersonal relationships. Learning what to work toward in relationships is as important as learning what to avoid. Thus, it is important to teach a student about the difference between appropriate irritation and anger, and the anger that has moved into behaviors that suggest that he or she has lost good judgment and control. Moreover, educators should talk about teen dating violence when, as so many already do, they teach conflict resolution skills.

ROLES FOR CHURCH-BASED PERSONNEL

Just as educators can be agents of accessibility and information, so too can church-based personnel. Survey responses indicate that teenage women were inclined to consult church personnel about problems in their dating relationships. However, church personnel, like educators, also need to be accessible, open, nonjudgmental, and informed about teen dating violence.

Just as it is sometimes difficult for teenage women to seek out teachers before or after school, church personnel will find it difficult to establish trusting relationships with teens if their only contacts with them are at crowded Sunday services—services that are attended more frequently by adults than by young people. Church youth groups, by contrast, offer less threatening opportunities for teens and adults to talk about a variety of topics including healthy and unhealthy dating relationships.

Despite the difficulties of establishing trusting relationships with teens at Sunday services, church personnel can convey information about teen dating violence in church bulletins and through sermons and homilies. Unfortunately, few clergy persons avail themselves of these resources or are trained to speak about widely acknowledged social problems such as alcoholism and substance abuse.[12] If clergy persons are so unprepared to deal with or fail to speak about the problems of addiction and substance abuse, the very "visible" perils to the integrity of family life, then one can only imagine that those who receive training about domestic abuse or teen dating violence, the "invisible perils," are even fewer in number. Alissa's story illustrates the damage that can be done to the well-being of a family, not only through substance abuse and addiction, but also through intimate partner violence. With increased attention from the clergy to all these social issues, and with more preaching on the topic, church-goers have a better chance to acknowledge and discuss the problems they en-counter in their personal lives. Moreover, preaching on these topics can pro-vide comfort to those in abusive relationships because they may be less embarrassed if they learn that they are not alone in confronting interpersonal violence. If spiritual leaders were more active in publicly addressing problems such as teen dating violence, then those in abusive relationships may become less reluctant to confide in them.

ROLES FOR THE LAW ENFORCEMENT COMMUNITY

In increasing numbers, police officers have visited schools to work with coun-selors and others who want to help students learn about teen dating violence. These officers, typically drawn from domestic violence units, are usually ac-quainted with and sympathetic to the problems of teens involved in abusive relationships. By contrast, law enforcement agents who work "on the street" and who are not familiar with the problems of teens involved in violent dating relationships, are often confused about how to respond to a teen's complaints. They also may be less sympathetic to a teen's accusations of abuse. For exam-ple, they may overlook or ignore abuse that is not physically apparent; or when sexual abuse or date rape occurs, they may castigate the young woman for her dress or behavior that made her "deserve" what she got. One police of-ficer, for example, reminded me that "The way these little girls go out, dressed like they are and such, they're really asking for it."

ROLES FOR THE COURTS

Not unlike many law enforcement officials, the courts are also somewhat con-fused about how to respond to allegations of teen dating violence. As discussed earlier, courts can issue orders of protection for minors who come before them when the minors are accompanied by a parent or guardian. However, such or-ders are limited and ineffective if the courts do not recognize that they need to work with schools where, as in Alejandra's case, it is virtually impossible to avoid contact with an abuser. For this reason, and because of the lack of clarity about whether, where, and how to bring cases to court when an abuser is confronted with his behavior, court officials sometimes focus more on the victim than they do on the accused. Further, a lack of clarity in the judicial system inclines attorneys and judges toward settling things outside of court. Such decisions are occasionally helpful. However, when an officer of the court does not take seriously the petition of the victim or her parents, courts often fail to protect the victim or bring justice to the offender. Even when they do address the behavior of the offender in a judicial setting, they are generally unable to do much to protect the victim or restore her sense of safety and well-being. What they usually can do is what they do best, that is, redress the crime by punishing the offender.

Unfortunately, society's "let's get him" emphasis on punishing the offender continues to deflect resources from programs designed to prevent the abuse in the first place. Social service agencies that have experienced personnel who can shelter and advise victims of abuse are generally not equipped or funded to levels where they can assist minors as easily as adults.

ROLES FOR THE RESEARCH COMMUNITY

All the parental support and legal services in the world, however, cannot help a young woman mired in abuse if she does not know that she is being abused. This is no small problem, the survey data suggest. A substantial number of the survey respondents could identify and would reject emotional violence. By contrast, they had more difficulty in identifying and rejecting hypothetical physically or sexually abusive behaviors. Also, they were unsure about what to do when someone forces them to have sex. They do not know that being forced to have sex, even if preceded by other occasions of intercourse, means that they have been raped.

The problem is even more serious for those who date regularly than for those who do not. Specifically, teenage women who date regularly are more ambivalent about rejecting patently abusive behavior than are those who have not dated within a year of the administration of the survey. Why the difference?

Such a question provides fertile ground for additional research. One hypothesis is that a nondater can only theoretically put herself in a situation and imagine how she might react. She *thinks she* would do what is right and reject a boyfriend who engages in inappropriate or patently physically or sexually abusive behaviors. A young dater, by contrast, is dealing with real situations. She clearly has something to lose, even if what she has to lose is an abuser.

Cognitive psychologists suggest that losses loom larger than gains and that the concepts of "psychological regret" and "selective perception" play major roles in decision making. Thus, "confronted with a choice between a certain loss [separating from an abusive boyfriend], on the one hand, and a probabilistic prospect of either avoiding that loss or of incurring a slightly larger one [either dating another boyfriend who is not abusive or having no boyfriend at all], on the other, people tend to opt for the chance of avoiding the loss" [not separating from an abusive boyfriend].[13] In the context of a dating relationship, for example, the prospect of losing a boyfriend, even if he is abusive, and then having either no boyfriend at all or possibly finding one who is not abusive, may dominate a teen's choice about whether to reject or remain with an abusive partner. Thus, choosing a prospective gain in the form of a hypothetical "Mr. Right" in the future is a difficult choice for a young woman in a violent dating relationship who has an abusive, but real, "Mr. Wrong."

Even when young teenage women first begin to experience abusive behavior, especially if it does not come in the early stages of their relationships, they may ignore it. Instead, again referring to the constructs of cognitive psychology, they may engage in selective perception or wishful thinking, "downplay/disregard conflicting evidence" [that they are being abused], and begin to seek "information that confirms existing notions" [their boyfriends really are not abusers because they had always been respectful before these violent outbursts].[14] They do not tend "to seek information that could disconfirm their hypotheses."[15] By contrast, they tend to assess the probabilities of good outcomes, the outcomes they desire, as being "higher than their state of knowledge justifies."[16]

Viewing the same decision-making process but from a different discipline, economists would argue that "sunk costs are sunk." Past costs of a bad decision are not a reason to justify paying additional costs in the future with the hope that, at some point, the calculus will shift and a bad decision will suddenly become a good one. From an economist's perspective, therefore, a young woman should make a decision about whether to separate from her partner *not* by using criteria based on the time and investment she has already "sunk" into the relationship but rather on the prospect that the potential gains of remaining in the relationship will outweigh the long-term costs. In an abusive relationship, however, cognitive psychologists would understand how difficult it would be for a teen to adopt an economic approach by cutting her losses and viewing "sunk costs as sunk." Further, they would understand her tendency to hold out hope that her situation will somehow change, thereby turning a bad investment in an abusive boyfriend into a good one.

Unfortunately, violence tends to escalate rather than diminish in abusive relationships. Thus, the prospects that future benefits will exceed future costs are low. In such situations, even an economist would probably recommend a decision to separate from an abuser!

Underlying Principles to Education and Prevention

Underlying the goals of education and prevention is the assumption that "it takes two to tango." That is, there are two parties to an abusive relationship. Thus, educational and prevention efforts, whether initiated or directed by the law enforcement community, the courts, social service providers, parents, educators, or church-based personnel, need to address the problems of both the abused and the abuser. In particular, what does such a principle imply?

First, to be truly helpful to those who are or who might be abused, especially teenage women, educational and prevention programs should focus on at least *several* of the factors that make young teenage women susceptible to becoming involved in unhealthy or violent relationships. Programs that focus exclusively on helping young women develop self-esteem, however, are only partly effective because such an orientation neglects other factors, such as witnessing abuse in the home, that also militate toward involvement in unhealthy relationships.

Second, educational and prevention programs should focus not only on the psycho-social development of young women but also young men. Such programs should recognize the impact of living in a "macho" culture that rewards self-interested, quick, controlling, and powerful responses not only in business, industry, and politics but also in human interactions. Without corresponding attention to the abuser's issues with power and control, programs that ignore the developmental needs of young men and, instead, focus exclusively on a young woman's self-esteem, may inadvertently reinforce the idea that teenage women themselves *cause* teen dating violence. Thus, a sort of insidious sexism may infiltrate well-intentioned programs by making teenage women feel responsible for controlling the behaviors of their male partners rather than encouraging young men to take responsibility for their own social behaviors. Thus, to avoid inadvertently castigating young women, even as adults try to help them avoid abuse, educational and prevention programs also need to address the problems of males who may become potential abusers. To do otherwise is to ignore the destructive capabilities of those who have an unhealthy need to exert power and control over others. Further, approaches that focus exclusively on young women deprive young men of the concern and care they need to become healthy partners in healthy intimate relationships later in life.

Prospective Policy Changes

What types of changes in public policy are needed to support the efforts of those communities of adults who want to prevent teen dating violence or help those who fall victim to it? Here, I join with others in making four policy recommendations.

CHANGE ATTITUDES AND PROCEDURES IN THE LAW ENFORCEMENT COMMUNITY

The attitudes of the law enforcement community need to change. The complaints of victims of teen dating violence must be taken seriously. Whether the issue is brought to the court's attention by the police, by the parents of the victim, or by the victim herself, the courts must regard teen dating violence as a crime if the facts, as best as the courts can ascertain, suggest that a crime has been committed. Officers of the court need to use discretion in dealing with questionable cases of abuse and should be allowed to work with all parties, including counselors and parents, to determine what is happening in alleged cases of abuse. They need latitude to negotiate an effective, safe, and workable understanding among all parties. They also need to make it clear that situations involving criminal behavior, such as harassment, stalking, and physical or sexual abuse, will be addressed in criminal rather than civil courts. Moreover, they need to make it clear that redress for criminal behavior will not be negotiated informally between the parties outside the courts simply because one or both of the parties is a minor. Rather, such behaviors need to be treated fairly and consistently by courts that take the problems of teenage women in abusive relationships as seriously as they do cases where adults are involved in domestic violence.

Essentially, such a policy recommendation requires two significant changes: one in clarifying the jurisdiction for teen dating violence; and the other in changing attitudes toward minors seeking orders of protection or other legal redress. In the words of the Center for Impact Research (CIR), courts need to be "friendlier" to minors so that domestic violence laws can protect both minors and adults.[17] Specifically, to avail themselves of court protection, teens must find it easier to access court resources without parental consent.

INCREASE ACCESSIBILITY TO SOCIAL SERVICES

Communities need to increase the number and accessibility of transitional housing services that are available to minors. Doing this would require three policy changes.

Reallocating Resources. Additional funds, whether from private or public sources, must be found and allocated to develop new facilities that admit minors, including pregnant minors or minors with children, who need shelter from abusers. It is imperative that temporary or long-term housing for teens who are pregnant or who have children be increased to help combat the extreme shortage of such housing. Because physical violence escalates in intimate partner relationships when pregnancy occurs, and because some, although not all, pregnant teens are living with their boyfriends, the lack of teen housing exacerbates the problem.[18] Without facilities such as transitional housing, teens are usually referred to shelters for homeless youths, settings which, because of many of the behavioral problems of homeless youths, are generally inappropriate for teenage women fleeing abusive relationships. Noting the effect of a lack of shelters that accept minors, a "transitional shelter for pregnant and parenting young adults (ages 18 to 21) located on the near northwest side [of Chicago] reported that staff had witnessed numerous incidences of teen mothers sleeping in cars and that it was turning away large numbers of pregnant and parenting teens."[19]

Relaxing Licensure Requirements. Local and state authorities need to relax licensure requirements so that minors can seek transitional or long-term housing while pursuing their educations away from their abusers. With or without the consent of parents, teens need refuge from dangerous situations, especially when there is evidence that physical and sexual dating violence may be occurring. In cases where parents do give consent for a teen to enter a domestic violence shelter, most teens will still be turned away because licensure requirements make it impossible for the shelter to accept the minor unless she has been legally emancipated by the courts. The plight of teenage women seeking shelter without parental support is equally frustrating because such licensed facilities are so few in number that they are virtually nonexistent. The CIR, for example, notes that in Illinois:

> In order to become licensed as a youth shelter through DCFS [Department of Children and Family Services], a facility must meet certain physical and staffing requirements. Most domestic violence shelters are not willing to become licensed due to perceived stringent requirements and the knowledge that the staff must be prepared to deal with an entirely different set of issues when dealing with minors.[20]

To better address the needs of teens, the CIR recommends that transitional living services be expanded "so that minors can be served beyond 120 days."[21] Moreover, such facilities need to create and then publicize a welcoming environment where young women will be respected as individuals and treated with dignity. Too often teenagers are scared off from approaching shelter facilities because they fear "too many rules" or that they will have no privacy.

Creating a "Partial Emancipation" Category. Although some states have already adopted such a category, the CIR recommends that a category of "partial emancipation" be created. This category would allow minors to "seek shelter provided by authorized youth service providers without securing parental consent in cases of family or domestic violence."[22] In other words, minors would be emancipated only for the purposes of obtaining shelter. Such laws are not without precedent. Alabama, Louisiana, and New York, for example, require parental notification when a teen seeks shelter, but "all specify that parents need not be notified when there are compelling reasons against it."[23]

EXPAND SOCIAL SERVICE ACCESS TO MINORS

Newly created shelters, and those that have altered their requirements to enable them to admit minors, also need to expand social, medical, and mental health services that are expressly designed for young teenage women, including those who are pregnant or caring for children. Research suggests that victims of teen dating violence are more inclined to access counseling services than other shelter services that may be available to them.[24] To be more helpful to teens, states that have not done so already should consider adopting a policy that extends the number of visits that a teen can make to a counselor without parental notification.

SHIFT FOCUS FROM PUNISHMENT TO PREVENTION

Implicit in the demand for educational and prevention programs at the elementary and secondary level is a corresponding shift in public policy. Specifically, resources need to focus on education and prevention programs, not simply on punishing the offender. Additional resources need to be directed toward funding centers where minors can be housed away from their abusers while still being able to continue their educations. Law enforcement agencies and the courts, many of which are making strong commitments to train personnel in domestic violence and abuse, need to recognize the existence of teen dating violence. Having recognized the problem, they need to take it seriously by learning the differences in the law as it applies to minors and adults. Underage victims need to be treated differently from adults because of the nature of abuse certainly, but also because of the differences in standing that each group has in the courts. Finally, courts need to routinize policies and procedures when parents, acting on behalf of their minor children, appeal for redress through the courts. Court officials need to understand that violence is violence. As such, when the violence occurs and either one or both of the parties to it are minors, then it needs to be treated as seriously, as consistently, and as criminally as cases where both partners are adults.

Making the Invisible Peril Visible: Just the Beginning

Many young teenage women seem to lack frames of reference for evaluating the behaviors of their dating partners. Because they often view abusive behaviors as isolated occurrences, they do not consider themselves in abusive *relationships*. On the contrary, abusive relationships happen to "others," especially if the "other" is an ethnic or racial minority. Thus, when teens first encounter abusive behavior, especially after they have dated for a while without incident, they feel "ambushed." They are stunned, have so little experience dating, and know very little about the existence of teen dating violence. Consequently, they do not know how to react to abuse when it happens to them. Because they are stunned and confused, they are often silent about what is happening to them. They are, as Alejandra told me, "left in silence."

Further, despite the breadth and depth of their dating experience, many young teenage women do not seem to know or understand what is happening to them when they are consistently being sworn at, kept waiting, or being "dissed" alone or in front of their friends. Even more amazing is their lack of understanding of what is happening to them physically or sexually. They do not know, for example, that "having sex" includes oral or anal intercourse. They do not know the physical and contextual behaviors that differentiate rape from sexual intercourse. They do not know that it is not only unsafe but also abusive when their partners refuse to use condoms. They do not know what stalking is, or that it is illegal, or that it can sometimes result in murder. They do not know that, once evident, violent behavior in dating partners is more likely to escalate than to subside. They do not know that it is virtually impossible for partners to change their abusers' behaviors.

Although teenage women may have been warned about date rape and know that they should keep an eye on their drinks at parties so no one slips anything into them, they do not know that being screamed at or berated is not only painful and embarrassing in the moment but that it also may be psychologically destructive in the long run. They may know a lot about how to use contraceptives and condoms, and may know about the availability of abortion counseling services when they want to terminate an unwanted pregnancy, but they do not know much about the resources that are available to help with basic problems in human relationships. Although they may be well versed in how to avoid sexually transmitted diseases, or make articulate arguments for or against same-sex relationships, they do not know that saying "No" or "Stop" has both moral and legal power. At a most basic level then, they know much about the mechanics of sex but little or nothing of its meaning and consequences.

In other words, they fall short in their understanding of the characteristics and dynamics of healthy interpersonal relationships. To quote T. S. Eliot in

"The Dry Salvages," many have "had the experience, but missed the meaning." Unfortunately, when they finally discover that they are in over their heads, they do not have information about the institutions and individuals who are willing and trained to help them. Thus, one of the first principles in education about teen dating violence is to assume that daters and nondaters alike know relatively little about what healthy dating relationships look like and how to maintain them. In addition, they do not know what teen dating violence looks like and what it means to experience it.

Why such ignorance and ambivalence? Why "left in silence?" Interviews with young teenage women suggest that many do not have clear expectations about what healthy dating relationships look like and what types of behaviors they should expect from their dating partners. Clearly, television is of little help in setting behavioral norms for young people. Adults may be relatively uninformed about the existence of teen dating violence and the ways that it differs from date rape. Personnel at local institutions such as schools, churches, social services, and law enforcement agencies may also be unaware of the problem or be relatively ill equipped to deal with the distinctive problems of minors. Where, then, will young teenage women learn how to differentiate healthy and appropriate behaviors from inappropriate or violent ones? When will they find their voices about what is happening to them so that they are *not* left in silence? How will the adults who care about teens help make the invisible peril *visible* so that it can be addressed in helpful and healthy ways?

The profound wisdom of noted French author, Antoine De Saint Exupery, immortalized in the classic *The Little Prince*, reminds us that "It is only with the heart that one can see rightly; what is essential is invisible to the eye." What has thus far remained "invisible to the eye" of many parents, educators, social service agencies, law enforcement agents, and court officers is the peril of teenage dating violence. We cannot change what we cannot see. Truly, if we can respond to what we know exists in our hearts, we can become powerful advocates for teens living this secret and perilous life.

Victims of teen dating violence ultimately see all too clearly that this abuse not only exists and imperils them, but also that it festers, grows, and endangers the lives of second and third generations. Alissa's heart grieves. "I find an anger in myself for allowing this to happen and for not putting a halt to it sooner. I would give anything to have been a stronger person, not only for myself, but also for my sons. I am tougher on myself than anyone could ever be."

Could Alissa have been a stronger person when she was a vulnerable teen, or even in later years as an adult who faced each day with fear and shame? Surely, Alissa made a number of mistakes for which she took responsibility and assumed the consequences. She could not frame what was happening to her, label it abuse, get out, and move on. Her perceptions of her partner may have been selective and, perhaps, immature. This research illustrates how these factors make a young woman vulnerable to becoming involved in an abusive relationship. However, this research also suggests that the entire blame should not be placed on Alissa and those like her.

Although Alissa made mistakes, she did not fail. Neither did Maggie, Alejandra, Lisa Santoro, and the thousands of others like them. Rather, they were failed: by cops who blew them off because "they deserved it"; by the courts that did not know how to deliver justice for teens because they were not adults; by the research community who finds the ethical demands so onerous that we too often shy away from collecting primary data from the teens themselves; and by the media that sensationalize the Columbines and ignore the insidious violence that picks off its victims one by one.

They were failed by parents and family members who did not ask questions or recognize the signs; by friends who could not help because they did not know what to do; by educators who are unable or who do not want to "hang around"; by church-based personnel who do not preach; and by social service agencies that want to help but often find that the law would not let them. Most of all, they were failed by a society that prefers punishment over education and prevention and, in its legal processes, ignores the developmental differences between children and adults and constrains young women and young men by promoting patriarchal roles and gender stereotypes that are unrealistic and often unhealthy.

Throughout this book, I have touched upon the preliminary steps that can help this invisible peril emerge from the periphery of our vision into full view as a visible peril—one that must be addressed for the Maggies, Alejandras, Lisas, and Alissas of our world. For these women, and for all teenage women, I hope that this confrontation with the invisible peril is "just the beginning."

METHODOLOGY

The general purpose of the research has been to examine the attitudes and experiences of female high school students in hypothetical or actual dating relationships. In particular, I examined the following:

- Respondents' perceptions about dating behaviors;
- Respondents' opinions about engaging in isolating behaviors while dating;
- Respondents' perceptions of self-worth;
- Respondents' willingness to seek the help of others if involved in a physically violent dating relationship;
- Respondents' willingness to seek help of others if involved in an emotionally violent dating relationship;
- Impediments to respondents' unwillingness to tell anyone about involvement in a physically violent dating relationship; and
- Respondents' experiences in dating relationships during the year preceding the administration of the survey.

To meet these objectives, the research methodology included survey research; interviews with high school teachers, counselors, and domestic violence counselors; and interviews of survivors of teen dating violence, including the family member of a young woman who had been murdered by a violent dating partner. A review of primary and secondary data and research, and materials from organizations combating domestic violence, was also essential.

Data Collection

The survey data analyzed for this book were collected during the fall 1999 and spring 2000 semesters.

Sample Construction

The sample consisted of 499 female high school juniors from 12 different parochial high schools in the Chicago area. Because respondents did not always respond to every question on the survey, the effective sample size was somewhat smaller depending on the particular question under scrutiny. For questions addressed to students who had dated within a year of the survey's administration, the sample size was usually about 390 respondents, again depending on the question. Overall, the nonresponse rate was low. Moreover, there did not appear to be a pattern to the unanswered questions.

EXTERNAL VALIDITY

As with many samples of teenagers participating in survey research, the sample for this research was a sample of convenience. Thus, the students in the sample were not randomly drawn. As such, they do not represent either the population of female high school juniors in the Chicago area or even the junior classes of the high schools that agreed to participate in the research.

The students who were subjects in the research were selected because they were the students of teachers who agreed to participate in the research and the Dating Violence Curriculum Intervention Project (DVCIP). Specifically, the principal of each school in the pilot project asked a teacher to participate. The teacher then selected one or two of his/her classes, usually depending on convenience and teaching schedule. In eleven of the schools, the teachers then designated one of his/her classes as the control group and one as the experimental group. The experimental group subsequently participated in the DCVIP while the control did not. In the twelfth school, participants were drawn from a voluntary after-school program rather than by classroom.

A pretest and a posttest were administered to both the experimental and control groups. The data for this research were drawn from the pretests of both the experimental and control group participants. Pretest/posttest comparisons of the DCVIP's efficacy and a comparison of responses in the control and experimental groups will be conducted at a later date.

Because the sample was not randomly drawn, it is impossible to generalize to a broader population of high school students, even to those from the Chicago area. Moreover, a student's choice not to participate in the survey (6 students), or his or her parents' refusal to give consent (10 students), could bias the responses if there were a common reason why either the parents or the students chose not to participate. Because sixteen students did not participate and ten more were absent the day the survey was administered, the effective size of the sample was reduced from 525 to 499. Thus, approximately 4 percent of the students who were asked to participate did not.

Was the sample racially and economically diverse? Because of the broad geographic distribution of the schools, the respondents from the 12 schools do represent a racially, ethnically, and economically diverse group of young women.

RELIABILITY

Because of the difficulties of administering surveys to minors, the survey was not pretested on high school students. It was, however, extensively reviewed by college students, colleagues, a domestic violence counselor, and members of DePaul University's Institutional Review Board.

When the survey was administered at each of the 12 sites, only a handful of respondents raised questions about the content of the survey. For the most part, these questions involved the meaning of "stalking."

Survey Construction

The purpose of the survey was threefold: first, to assess respondents' attitudes toward different dating experiences, including those of an emotionally, physically, or sexually violent nature; second, to describe and to measure the respondents' experiences of emotional, physical, and sexual abuse; and third, to determine whether and where respondents would go were they to become involved in violent dating relationships.

The survey instrument consisted of seven sets of questions, most of which were in a Likert Scale format where respondents were asked to indicate frequency of occurrence or the strength of their feelings about a number of dating behaviors. For example, I asked, "If [a respondent] were involved in a physically violent dating relationship, that is, if a boyfriend were hitting, shoving, or punching" her, whom might she tell? Would she "definitely tell," "might tell," or "definitely would not tell" someone about the behavior? Alternatively, would she respond that she did "not know" what she would do?

In the first set of questions, all student respondents, regardless of whether they had ever dated or were currently dating, were asked to indicate which category of a Likert Scale most closely reflected their opinions about dating or dating behaviors. Within this first set of questions was a subset of questions designed to determine the following:

- a respondent's tendency to isolate herself from others while dating;
- a respondent's willingness to talk openly with others about conflicts with others while dating;
- a respondent's tolerance for behaviors that could be construed as emotionally/psychologically, physically, or sexually violent;

- a respondent's self-assessment about her ability to recognize or remove herself from a violent dating relationship, however she defined it;
- the types of resources a respondent thinks she could access if she were to become involved in a violent dating relationship;
- some indicators of a respondent's level of self-esteem.

In the second and third sets of parallel questions, respondents were asked whom they would seek out if they were to become involved in a physically or emotionally abusive relationship with their boyfriends. Here, a physically violent relationship was characterized by a boyfriend's "hitting, shoving, or punching." An emotionally abusive relationship was described as a boyfriend's stalking or swearing at his date, trying to stop her from seeing her friends, or trying to control what she does with her time. Would they, for example, be more or less inclined to tell a teacher? A counselor? A peer? A parent? Others?

In the fourth set of questions, all respondents were asked to think about the reasons that would inhibit them from telling anyone if they became involved in a physically violent relationship. For example, were they fearful of retaliation? Were they embarrassed? Did they think that people would ignore their predicament?

The fifth set of questions focused on separating out those respondents who had dated within a year of the survey's administration from those who had not dated. Specifically, it asked those who had dated to describe their dating experiences, both in character and frequency.

In the sixth set of questions, also directed toward those who had dated during the past year, I asked respondents directly whether they had been abused in a dating relationship. The seventh set of questions was designed to collect demographic data and information about overall dating patterns including the frequency of dating and whether the respondent had dated the same boy or different boys throughout the year.

Obtaining Consent

As discussed in Chapter Four, the consent of several individuals and institutions was needed before the survey could be administered. First, the survey and the accompanying consent form were reviewed and approved by the Institutional Review Board of DePaul University, where I was a faculty member at the time that the survey was administered. This was especially important not only because of the sensitive nature of the questions, but also because the survey respondents were minors. Moreover, each of the women needed active consent from a guardian in order to participate. Additionally, each student who received active consent was encouraged to decide for herself whether she wished to participate in the survey. Surveys were confidential unless students chose to reveal themselves by writing their names on the surveys. If a student put her name on a survey, then, she was told in advance, her survey would be shown to the school counselor. The school counselor would, in turn, seek out the student to talk with her to determine if the student was involved in a questionable relationship. If so, the counselor would then contact the student's parents. In only one case did a student identify herself by name on a survey. Subsequently, the counselor was informed and a helpful conversation between the teen and the counselor ensued.

Statistical Measures

Because of the ordinal nature of Likert Scale data, frequency distributions were the method of choice for descriptive statistics. In cases where comparisons were important, Chi-square analyses were used and levels of statistical significance were noted. When correlations were required, both Spearman's and Pearson's coefficients were generated, and the direction, level of strength, and statistical significance were analyzed. Both measures yielded similar results.

The Dating Violence Curriculum Intervention Project

The Dating Violence Curriculum Intervention Project (DVCIP) is an extended and intensive examination of the problem of teen dating violence. Using a novel that describes how a young teenage woman became involved in a violent dating relationship when she was in high school, teachers and counselors worked together in each classroom of students to help students identify and discuss different dimensions of such relationships. Through reading, discussion, and the sharing of personal experiences, students learned to identify the behaviors of abusive partners that were precursors to an abusive relationship. In addition, they learned to identify the appropriate ownership of the problem—allocating responsibility for the violent behavior to the abuser, not the victim. Finally, they learned how to help themselves and their friends seek help in separating from abusive boyfriends. Both the book, Clark's *The Breakable Vow*, and a teaching manual are available from Adams Press, 500 N. Michigan Avenue, Suite 1920, Chicago, Illinois 60611–3794, or info@adamspresschicago.com.

In preparation for both the administration of the survey and the DVCIP, each high school sent participating teachers and counselors to a one-day training workshop. At this workshop, both the faculty member and the counselor were introduced to the problem of teen dating violence, its characteristics, and the characteristics of the abuser. They learned various ways to identify teen dating violence and also discussed how to respond to students having such problems. Further, they were introduced to both the novel and the curriculum and accompanying manual, and then worked through some of the exercises in the curriculum.

When the curriculum was actually introduced to the students, both the teacher and the counselor were present or available throughout the class sessions. In some cases, the teacher and the counselor team-taught the curriculum. In other cases, the teacher worked through the curriculum with the students while the counselor was available for crisis intervention. Both teachers and counselors reported being very satisfied with the curriculum and offered some suggestions about how they would improve the curriculum were they to teach it again.

NOTES

Introduction: The Invisible Peril

1. The Illinois Domestic Violence Act, 1986 (750ILCS60/103)[Section 103] (1).
2. Jay G. Silverman, Anita Raj, Lorelei A. Mucci, and Jeanne E. Hathaway, "Dating Violence Against Adolescent Girls and Associated Substance Abuse Use, Unhealthy Weight Control, Sexual Risk Behavior, Pregnancy, and Suicidality," *Journal of the American Medical Association*, 286.5 (2001): 572–579.

Chapter 1: The Faces of Teen Dating Violence

1. Unless noted by last name, all of the names of the individuals who contributed to this work by sharing their stories with me have been changed to protect them from potential retaliation from their former boyfriends. All of their contributions were used with permission, and I want to thank them because this project would have suffered greatly without the detail they have provided.
2. Tom Santoro, "Dear Lisa Dating Violence Prevention Program," interview by author, 12 January 2001.
3. Although Tom Santoro and the "Dear Lisa" dating violence prevention program are based in the Chicago area, Tom has appeared on the Oprah Winfrey and Montel Williams shows. He is available to take his message about teen dating violence across the country with the hope of "making a difference in just one person's life." Tom welcomes being contacted at 708.863.LISA.

Chapter 2: A Profile of the Invisible Peril

1. Kerry Wells, *Training Manual on Stalking* (San Diego: San Diego Stalking Strike Force, 1997), 2.
2. Ibid.
3. The Illinois Domestic Violence Act, 1986.

4. Ibid., 7, 9, 14.
5. Marquette County Michigan, *Marquette County Law Enforcement Domestic Violence Policy and Procedure* (Michigan: Marquette County: May 1995; revised December 1995, and February 1997), quoted in *Domestic Violence: Prosecutors Take the Lead* (Cambridge: The American Prosecutors Research Institute, 1997), 69.
6. Stacy L. Brustin, "Legal Responses to Teen Dating Violence," *Family Law Quarterly* 29.2 (1995): 335.
7. Carole A. Sousa, "Teen Dating Violence: The Hidden Epidemic," *Family and Conciliation Courts Review* 37 (July 1999): 357.
8. Minnesota Program Development, Inc., *Power and Control and Equality Wheels* (Duluth: Domestic Abuse Intervention Project, 1999). Used with permission. The Domestic Abuse and Intervention Project materials, including poster-size Power and Control and Equality Wheels, were developed by battered women in Duluth. These materials are part of an educational curriculum *Power and Control: Tactics of Men Who Batter*, available from Minnesota Program Development, Inc., 202 East Superior Street, Duluth, MN 55802.
9. Ibid.
10. Project for Victims of Family Violence, Inc., *Signs to Look for in a Battering Personality* (Fayetteville, AR: Project for Victims of Family Violence, Inc., n.d.). Used with permission.
11. Ibid.
12. Diane Bedrosian, untitled pamphlet (Homewood, IL: The South Suburban Family Shelter, n.d.).
13. Ibid.
14. Barbara J. Hart, "Beyond the 'Duty to Warn': A Therapist's 'Duty to Protect' Battered Women and Children." In *Feminist Perspectives on Wife Abuse*, 234–248, eds. Kersti Yllö and Michele Bograd (Beverly Hills: Sage, 1992).
15. Ibid.
16. Evan Stark and Anne Flitcraft, "Women and Children at Risk: A Feminist Perspective on Child Abuse," *International Journal of Health Services* 18.1 (1988): 97–118.
17. Wells, 15.
18. Ibid.

Chapter 3: Current Teen Dating Violence Policy

1. Wells, *Training Manual on Stalking*.
2. Sousa, *Teen Dating Violence*, 359.
3. Ibid., 24, 25.
4. The Illinois Domestic Violence Act, 1986, 6.
5. Illinois Compiled Statutes Families Emancipation and Mature Minors Act (750ILCS30/32).
6. Sousa, *Teen Dating Violence*, 371.
7. Brustin, "Legal Responses," 332.
8. Ibid., 332.
9. Ibid., 338.
10. Ibid., 332.
11. Ibid., 343–344.
12. Ibid., 344.

13. Ibid.
14. Helen M. Marcy and Monica Martinez, *Helping with Domestic Violence: Legal Barriers to Serving Teens in Illinois* (Chicago: Center for Impact Research, 2000).
15. Ibid.
16. Seth C. Kalichman, *Mandated Reporting of Suspected Child Abuse: Ethics, Law, and Policy in Protecting Human Subjects* (Washington, D.C.: American Psychological Association, 1993), 2.
17. Ibid., 11.
18. Child Abuse Prevention, Adoption, and Family Services Act of 1974, U.S.C.S. Sections (3) 5101–5115 (1979, Cum. Supp., 1988), cited in *Mandated Reporting of Suspected Child Abuse: Ethics, Law and Policy in Protecting Human Subjects*, Seth C. Kalichman (Washington, D.C.: American Psychological Association, 1993), 11–12.
19. A. H. McCoid, "The Battered Child and Other Assaults Upon the Family," *Minnesota Law Review* 50 (1965): 1–58, cited in *Mandated Reporting of Suspected Child Abuse: Ethics, Law and Policy in Protecting Human Subjects*, Seth C. Kalichman (Washington, D.C.: American Psychological Association, 1993), 11.
20. Even if teen dating violence were legally considered to be child abuse, however, research suggests that mandated reporters are still reluctant to report these cases to state child welfare authorities in spite of a number of penalties that can be levied on them. Many accept these risks because they believe that such reporting requirements limit confidentiality and an individual's privacy in a professional therapeutic relationship. Thus, laws that require reporting suspected child abuse and neglect in professional contests sometimes conflict with basic professional standards. See W. Curran, "Failure to Diagnose Battered Child Syndrome," *New England Journal of Medicine* 296 (1977): 795–796; and A. Hedberg, "Child Abuse Reporting—A Personal and Professional Trauma and Trial," discussion session, San Francisco: American Psychological Association (August 1991); each cited in *Mandated Reporting of Suspected Child Abuse: Ethics, Law and Policy in Protecting Human Subjects*, Seth C. Kalichman (Washington, D.C.: American Psychological Association, 1993), 3.

Chapter 4: Teen Dating Violence Research

1. Craig A. Perkins, "Age Patterns of Victims of Serious Crime," *Bureau of Justice Statistics Report* (Washington, D.C.: U.S. Department of Justice, Office of Justice Programs, September 1997) <http://www.ojp.usdoj.gov/bjs/pub/ascii/asvsvc.txt> (1 February 2001).
2. Patricia G. Tjaden and Nancy Thoennes, "Prevalence, Incidence, and Consequences of Violence Against Women: Findings from the National Violence Against Women Survey," *National Institute of Justice Centers for Disease Control and Prevention Research in Brief* (Washington, D.C.: U.S. Department of Justice, Office of Justice Programs, November 1998) <http://ncjrs.org/pdffiles/172837.pdf> (6 December 2001), 2.
3. Ibid., 6.
4. Ronet Bachman and Linda E. Saltzman, "National Crime Victimization Survey: Violence Against Women: Estimates from the Redesigned Survey," *Bureau of Justice Statistics Special Report* (Washington, D.C.: U.S. Department of Justice, Office of Justice Programs, August 1995).
5. Bachman and Saltzman, 3.

6. Diane Craven, "Sex Differences in Violent Victimizations, 1994," *Bureau of Justice Statistics Special Report* (Washington, D.C.: U.S. Department of Justice, September 1997), 1.

7. Bachman and Saltzman, 3.

8. Ibid., 8.

9. Bachman and Saltzman, 4.

10. Craven, 5.

11. Ibid.

12. Bachman and Saltzman, 4.

13. Ibid.

14. Ibid.

15. Bradley-Angle House, "Teen Dating Violence Happens," *Programs to End Domestic Violence* <http://www.bradleyangle.org/For_Teens/teen_datingviolence.htm> (17 April 2002), n.p.

15. Ibid.

16. Ibid.

17. Denise Wittmer, "Dating Violence," *Parenting of Adolescents* <http:// parentingteens.about. com/library/weekly/aa041900a.htm?terms=dating+violence> (6 December 2001): n.p.

18. Ibid.

19. Ibid.

20. Sheila Kuehl, "Legal Remedies for Teen Dating Violence," in *Dating Violence: Young Women in Danger*, ed. Barrie Levy (Seattle: Seal Press, 1991), 209–220.

21. Barrie Levy, ed., *Dating Violence: Young Women in Danger* (Seattle: Seal Press, 1991), 4.

22. David R. Jezl, Christian E. Molidor, and Tracy Wright, "Physical, Sexual, and Psychological Abuse in High School Dating Relationships: Prevalence Rates and Self Esteem Issues," *Child and Adolescent Social Work Journal* 13 (February, 1996): 69–87.

23. Christian E. Molidor and Richard Tolman, "Gender and Contextual Factors in Adolescent Dating Violence," *Violence Against Women* 4.1 (1998): 180–194.

24. Marlies Suderman and Peter Jaffe, "Violence in Teen Dating Relationships: Evaluation of a Large Scale Primary Intervention Program: Executive Summary" (London: London Family Court Clinic, n.d.).

25. Libby Bergman, "Dating Violence Among High School Students," *Social Work* 37.1 (1992): 21–27, cited in "Gender and Contextual Factors in Adolescent Dating Violence," Christian E. Molidor and Richard Tolman, *Violence Against Women* 4 (April 1998): 180–194.

26. Bachman and Saltzman, "National Crime Victimization Survey," 1.

27. Ibid.

28. National Center for Injury Prevention and Control, *Intimate Partner and Sexual Violence, Fact Book for the Year 2000: Working To Prevent Injury and Control in the United States* (Washington, D.C.: Center for Disease Control and Prevention, 12 July 2000) <http:// www.cdc.gov/ncipc/pub-res/FactBook/partner.htm> (6 December 2001), n.p.

29. Michael W. Wiederman, "Sexuality Research, Institutional Review Boards, and Subject Pools," in *Protecting Human Subjects: Departmental Subject Pools and Institutional Review Boards*, eds. Garvin Chastain and R. Eric Landrum (Washington, D.C.: American Psychological Association, 1999), 202.

30. Ibid.

31. Ibid.

32. Lynn Phillips, *The Girls Report: What We Know and Need to Know About Growing up Female* (New York: National Council for Research on Women, 1998), 45.

33. Wiederman, "Sexuality Research," 208.
34. Ibid.
35. Ibid.
36. Donald L. Mosher, "Balancing the Rights of Subjects, Scientists, and Society: 10 Principles for Human Subjects Committees," *The Journal of Sex and Marital Therapy* 24 (1988): 378–385, cited in "Sexuality Research, Institutional Review Boards, and Subject Pools," Michael W. Wiederman, in *Protecting Human Subjects: Departmental Subject Pools and Institutional Review Boards*, 201–219, eds. Garvin Chastain and R. Eric Landrum (Washington, D.C.: American Psychological Association, 1999), 209.
37. Wiederman, "Sexuality Research," 208.

Chapter 5: Emotionally Abusive Dating Behavior

1. Percentages sometimes do not add up to 100 percent due to rounding error.
2. The only indicators of emotional abuse that were not correlated at a .05 level of statistical significance were the relations between the experience of emotional abuse and each of the following: experiences of stalking, not being consulted about what to do on a date, and worrying that the boyfriend would hurt someone in the family if a break-up occurred. The data were ordinal level and both Pearson's correlation coefficient and Spearman's rho tests yielded similar results.

Chapter 6: Physically and Sexually Abusive Behavior

1. I am grateful to Kathy Clarke for telling this story and recommend her book *The Breakable Vow* (Chicago: Adams Press, 2000) to those interested in using a work of fiction as a basis for a dating violence prevention program. A teacher's manual may also be purchased in conjunction with the book.
2. These findings should be viewed with caution insofar as some of the cells in the X^2 test had a small number of cases. Moreover, research about the relationship between race or ethnicity and domestic violence is inconclusive. Bachman and Saltzman, "National Crime," 1995, for example, conclude that all races are equally vulnerable to violence against intimates. Other studies that do find some statistically significant relationship between race/ethnicity and the incidence or levels of domestic violence frequently qualify their results because of relatively small numbers of racial/ethnic minorities in the sample or because of the inability to hold constant other factors such as income.
3. See Stephanie A. Sanders and June Machover Reinisch, "Would You Say You 'Had Sex' If . . . ?" *Journal of the American Medical Association* 281.3 (January 1999): 275–277.

Chapter 7: Finding a Way Out

1. Carolyn M. Ball, *Claiming Your Self Esteem* (Berkeley: Celestial Arts Publishing, 1990).
2. Quincy Model Domestic Abuse Program (QMDAP), *Police Response to Domestic Violence Manual* (Quincy, MA: Quincy Model Domestic Abuse Program, n.d.), 9.

3. Peter G. Jaffe, Marlies Suderman, Deborah Reitzel, and Steve M. Killip, "An Evaluation of a Secondary School Primary Prevention Program on Violence in Intimate Relationships," *Violence and Victims* 7.2 (1992): 129–146.

4. Linda McLeod, *Battered, Not Broken: Preventing Wife Beating in Canada* (Ottawa: Canadian Advisory Council on the Status of Women, 1987), cited in "An Evaluation of a Secondary School Primary Prevention Program on Violence in Intimate Relationships," Peter G. Jaffe, Marlies Suderman, Deborah Reitzel, and Steve M. Killip, *Violence and Victims* 7.2 (1992): 129–146.

5. Bachman and Saltzman, "National Crime," 1995, found that women between the ages of 19 and 29 in families with incomes under $10,000 were more likely to be victims of violence by intimates.

6. QMDAP, Police Response, 10.

7. Gerald T. Hotaling and David B. Sugarman, "An Analysis of Risk Factors in Husband to Wife Violence: The Current State of Knowledge," *Victims and Violence* 1.2 (1986): 102–124.

8. QMDAP, 10.

9. Ibid.

10. Ibid., 13.

11. Jacquelyn C. Campbell, "'If I Can't Have You No One Can': Power and Control in Homicides of Female Partners," in *Femicide: The Politics of Woman Killing*, 99–113, eds. J. Radford and Diane E. H. Russell, New York: Twayne Publishers, 1992; and Cynthia K. Gillespie, *Justifiable Homicide* (Columbus: Ohio State University Press, 1989), each cited in "Domestic Violence: A National Curriculum for Family Preservation Practitioners," Susan Schechter and Anne L. Ganley (State of Michigan Department of Social Services, 1995), 24.

12. Angela Frederick, "Adolescent Dating Violence," *Nursing Spectrum* 14.20 (2001): 22–25.

13. S. F. Lewis and William Fremouw, "Dating Violence: A Critical Review of the Literature," *Clinical Psychology Review* 21 (2001): 105–127, cited in "Adolescent Dating Violence," Angela Frederick, *Nursing Spectrum* 14.20 (2001): 22–25.

Chapter 8: (Not the) Conclusion

1. Silverman et al., "Dating Violence Against," 574.

2. Ibid., 578.

3. Tener Goodwin Veenema, "Children's Exposure to Community Violence," *Journal of Nursing Scholarship* 33.2 (2001): 171.

4. National Women Abuse Prevention Project, *Sad Is How You Feel When Mom Is Being Beaten* (Texas Department of Human Services: Media Services, May, 1997): n.p.

5. Ibid.

6. Vangie A. Foshee, George F. Linder, Karl E. Bauman et al., "The Safe Dates Project: Theoretical Basis, Evaluation Design, and Selected Based Findings," *American Journal of Preventive Medicine* 12.5 supp. (1996): 39–47 and Sarah Avery-Leaf, M. Cascardi, K. D. O'Leary, and A. Cano, "Efficacy of a Dating Violence Prevention Program on Attitudes Justifying Aggression, *Journal of Adolescent Health* 21 (1997): 11–17, each cited in "Dating Violence Against Adolescent Girls and Associated Substance Abuse Use, Unhealthy Weight Control, Sexual Risk Behavior, Pregnancy, and

Suicidality," Jay G. Silverman, Anita Raj, Lorelei A. Mucci and Jeanne E. Hathaway, *Journal of the American Medical Association* 286.5 (2001): 572–579.

7. Judith Mackay, *The Penguin Atlas of Human Sexual Behavior* (New York: Penguin Putnam Inc., 2000), 30.

8. Dating Violence Prevention Project of the Battered Women's Shelter, *Teen Safety Plan* (San Antonio: Battered Women's Shelter, n.d.).

9. Ibid.

10. See Clarke.

11. Through the sharing that occurs over literature, teens and facilitators can sometimes talk more candidly about their reactions to characters in the novel, who may, in fact, be mirrors of their own dating problems. Though discussions over novels are standard practice in literature classes, when used for therapeutic purposes the technique is called "bibliotherapy." There are mixed results on the efficacy of bibliotherapy, although nursing professionals and some educators think that the technique, when used by trained individuals, can be effective in helping "(1) to develop an individual's self-concept; (2) to increase an individual's understanding of human behavior or motivations; (3) to foster an individual's honest self-appraisal; (4) to provide a way for a person to find interests outside of self; (5) to relieve emotional or mental pressure; (6) to show an individual that he or she is not the first or only person to encounter such a problem; (7) to show an individual that there is more than one solution to a problem; (8) to help a person discuss a problem more freely; and (9) to help an individual plan a constructive course of action to solve a problem." Nola Kortner Aiex, *Bibliotherapy* (Bloomington: ERIC Clearinghouse on Reading, English, and Communication Digest 82 (June 1993) <http://www.indiana.edu/~eric_rec/ieo/ digests/d82.html> (1 January 2002).

12. Joseph Califano, Jr., "Statement on Release," *So Help Me God: Substance Abuse, Religion, and Spirituality* (Washington, D.C.: National Center on Addiction and Substance Abuse, 14 November 2001).

13. Robin M. Hogarth, *Judgment and Choice: The Psychology of Decision* (Chichester: John Wiley and Sons, 1985), 72.

14. Ibid., 166.

15. Ibid., 82.

16. Ibid., 170.

17. Marcy and Martinez, *Helping with Domestic Violence*, 26.

18. Ibid.

19. Ibid., 10.

20. Ibid., 8.

21. Ibid., 25.

22. Ibid., 14.

23. Ibid., 13.

24. Ibid.

BIBLIOGRAPHY

Aiex, Nola Kortner. *Bibliotherapy*. Bloomington: ERIC Clearinghouse on Reading, English, and Communication Digest 82 (June 1993) <www.indiana. edu/~eric_rec/ ieo/ digests/d82.html> 1 January 2002.

American Prosecutors Research Institute. *Domestic Violence: Prosecutors Take the Lead*. Cambridge: American Prosecutors Research Institute, 1997.

Avery-Leaf, Sarah, M. Cascardi, K. D. O'Leary, and A. Cano. "Efficacy of a Dating Violence Prevention Program on Attitudes Justifying Aggression." *Journal of Adolescent Health* 21 (1997): 11–17.

Bachman, Ronet, and Linda E. Saltzman. "National Crime Victimization Survey: Violence Against Women: Estimates from the Redesigned Survey." *Bureau of Justice Statistics Special Report*. Washington, D.C.: U.S. Department of Justice, Office of Justice Programs, 1995.

Ball, Carolyn M. *Claiming Your Self-Esteem*. Berkeley: Celestial Arts Publishing, 1990.

Bedrosian, Diane. Untitled Pamphlet. Homewood, IL: South Suburban Family Shelter, n.d.

Bergman, Libby. "Dating Violence Among High School Students." *Social Work* 37.1 (1992): 21–27.

Bradley-Angle House. "Teen Dating Violence Happens." *Programs to End Domestic Violence*. <http://www.bradleyangle.org/For_Teens/teen_dating_violence.htm> 17 April 2002.

Brustin, Stacy L. "Legal Responses to Teen Dating Violence." *Family Law Quarterly* 29.2 (1995): 331–366.

Califano, Joseph, Jr. "Statement on Release." *So Help Me God: Substance Abuse, Religion, and Spirituality*. Washington, D.C.: National Center on Addiction and Substance Abuse, 2001.

Campbell, Jacquelyn C. "'If I Can't Have You No One Can': Power and Control in Homicides of Female Partners." In *Femicide: The Politics of Woman Killing*, eds. J. Radford and Diane E. H. Russell, 99–113. New York: Twayne Publishers, 1992.

Chastain, Garvin, and R. Eric Landrum, eds. *Protecting Human Subjects: Departmental*

Subject Pools and Institutional Review Boards. Washington, D.C.: American Psychological Association, 1999.

Child Abuse Prevention, Adoption, and Family Services Act of 1974, U.S.C.S. Sections (3) 5101–5115 (1979, Cum. Supp., 1988).

Clarke, Kathryn. *The Breakable Vow.* Chicago: Adams Press, 2000.

Craven, Diane. "Sex Differences in Violent Victimizations, 1994." *Bureau of Justice Statistics Special Report.* Washington, D.C.: U.S. Department of Justice, 1997.

Curran, W. "Failure to Diagnose Battered Child Syndrome." *New England Journal of Medicine* 296 (1977): 795–796.

Dating Violence Prevention Project of the Battered Women's Shelter. *Teen Safety Plan.* San Antonio: Battered Women's Shelter, n.d.

Foshee, Vangie A., George F. Linder, Karl E. Bauman, et al. "The Safe Dates Project: Theoretical Basis, Evaluation, Design, and Selected Base Findings." *American Journal of Preventive Medicine* 12.5 Supp. (1996): 39–47.

Frederick, Angela. "Adolescent Dating Violence." *Nursing Spectrum* 14.20 (2001): 22–25.

Gillespie, Cynthia K. *Justifiable Homicide.* Columbus: Ohio State University Press, 1989.

Hart, Barbara J. "Beyond the 'Duty to Warn:' A Therapist's 'Duty to Protect' Battered Women and Children." In *Feminist Perspectives on Wife Abuse*, eds. Kersti Yllö and Michele Bograd, 234–248. Beverly Hills: Sage, 1992.

Hedberg, A. "Child Abuse Reporting—a Personal and Professional Trauma and Trial." Discussion Session. San Francisco: American Psychological Association, 1991.

Hogarth, Robin M. *Judgment and Choice: The Psychology of Decision.* Chichester: John Wiley and Sons, 1985.

Hotaling, Gerald T., and David B. Sugarman. "An Analysis of Risk Factors in Husband to Wife Violence: The Current State of Knowledge." *Violence and Victims* 1.2 (1986): 102–124.

Illinois General Assembly. Domestic Violence Act of 1986. (750ILCS60)/103) [Section 103].

Illinois General Assembly. Compiled Statutes Families Emancipation and Mature Minors Act. (750ILCS30/32).

Jaffe, Peter, Marlies Suderman, Deborah Reitzel, and Steve M. Killip. "An Evaluation of a Secondary School Prevention Program on Violence in Intimate Relationships." *Violence and Victims* 7.2 (1992): 129–146.

Jezl, David R., Christian E. Molidor, and Tracy L. Wright. "Physical, Sexual, and Psychological Abuse in High School Dating Relationships: Prevalence Rates and Self-Esteem Issues." *Child and Adolescent Social Work Journal* 13.1 (1996): 69–87.

Kalichman, Seth C. *Mandated Reporting of Suspected Child Abuse: Ethics, Law, and Policy in Protecting Human Subjects.* Washington, D.C.: American Psychological Association, 1993.

Kuehl, Sheila. "Legal Remedies for Teen Dating Violence." In *Dating Violence: Young Women in Danger,* ed. Barrie Levy, 209–220. Seattle: Seal Press, 1991.

Levy, Barrie, ed. *Dating Violence: Young Women in Danger*. Seattle: Seal Press, 1991.

Lewis, S. F., and William Fremouw. "Dating Violence: A Critical Review of the Literature." *Clinical Psychology Review* 21 (2001): 105–127.

Mackay, Judith. *The Penguin Atlas of Human Sexual Behavior*. New York: Penguin Putnam Inc., 2000.

Marcy, Helen M., and Monica Martinez. *Helping with Domestic Violence: Legal Barriers to Serving Teens in Illinois*. Chicago: Center for Impact Research, 2000.

Marquette County, Michigan. *Marquette County Law Enforcement Domestic Violence Policy and Procedure*. 1995. Michigan: Marquette County, 1997.

McLeod, Linda. *Battered, Not Broken: Preventing Wife Beating in Canada*. Ottawa: Canadian Advisory Council on the Status of Women, 1987.

McCoid, A. H. "The Battered Child and Other Assaults upon the Family." *Minnesota Law Review* 50 (1965): 1–58.

Minnesota Program Development. Inc. *Power and Control and Equality Wheels*. Duluth: Domestic Abuse Intervention Project, 1999.

Molidor, Christian E., and Richard Tolman. "Gender and Contextual Factors in Adolescent Dating Violence." *Violence Against Women* 4 (April, 1998): 180–194.

Mosher, Donald L. "Balancing the Rights of Subjects, Scientists, and Society: 10 Principles for Human Subjects Committees." *Journal of Marital Therapy* 21 (1988): 378–385.

National Center for Injury Prevention and Control. *Intimate Partner and Sexual Violence, Fact Book for the Year 2000: Working to Prevent Injury and Control in the United States*. Washington, D.C.: Center for Disease Control and Prevention (2000) <http: // www.cdc.gov/ncipc/pub-res/FactBook/partner.htm> 6 December 2001.

National Women Abuse Prevention Project. *Sad Is How You Feel When Mom Is Being Beaten*. Texas Department of Human Services: Media Services, 1997.

Perkins, Craig A. "Age Patterns of Victims of Serious Crimes." *Bureau of Justice Statistics Report*. Washington, D.C.: U.S. Department of Justice, Office of Justice Programs (September 1997) <http:// www. ojp.usdoj.gov/bjs/pub/ascii/asvsvc.txt> 1 February 2001.

Phillips, Lynn. *The Girls Report: What We Know and Need to Know about Growing up Female*. New York: National Council for Research on Women, 1998.

Project for Victims of Family Violence, Inc. *Signs to Look for in a Battering Personality*. Fayetteville: AR: Project for Victims of Family Violence, Inc., n.d.

Quincy Model Domestic Abuse Program (QMDAP). *Police Response to Domestic Violence Manual*. Quincy, MA: Quincy Model Domestic Abuse Program, n.d.

Radford Jill, and Diana E. H. Russell. *Femicide: The Politics of Woman Killing*. New York: Twayne Publishers, 1992.

Sanders, Stephanie A., and June Machover Reinisch. "Would You Say You 'Had Sex' If . . . ?" *Journal of the American Medical Association* 281.3 (1999): 275–277.

Santoro, Tom. "Dear Lisa Dating Violence Prevention Program." Interview by author. LaGrange, IL, 12 January 2001.

Schechter, Susan, and Anne L. Ganley. *Domestic Violence: A National Curriculum for Family Preservation Practitioners*. Lansing: State of Michigan Department of Social Services, 1995.

Silverman, Jay G., Anita Raj, Lorelei A. Mucci, and Jane E. Hathaway. "Dating Violence Against Adolescent Girls and Associated Substance Abuse, Unhealthy Weight Control, Sexual Risk Behavior, Pregnancy, and Suicidality." *Journal of the American Medical Association* 286.5 (2001): 572–579.

Sousa, Carole A. "Teen Dating Violence: The Hidden Epidemic." *Family and Conciliation Courts Review* 37 (July 1999): 356–372.

Stark, Evan, and Anne Flitcraft. "Women and Children at Risk: A Feminist Perspective on Child Abuse." *International Journal of Health Services* 18.1 (1988): 97–118.

Suderman, Marlies, and Peter Jaffe. *Violence in Teen Dating Relationships: Evaluation of a Large Scale Primary Intervention Program: Executive Summary.* London: London Family Court Clinic, n.d.

Tjaden, Patricia, and Nancy Thoennes. "Prevalence, Incidence, and Consequences of Violence Against Women: Findings From the National Violence Against Women Survey." *National Institute of Justice Centers for Disease Control and Prevention Research in Brief* (Washington D.C.: U.S. Department of Justice Office of Justice Programs November 1998) <http://ncjrs.org/pdffiles/172837.pdf> 6 December 2001.

Veenema, Tener Goodwin. "Children's Exposure to Community Violence." *Journal Nursing Scholarship* 33.2 (2001): 167–173.

Wells, Kerry. *Training Manual on Stalking.* San Diego: San Diego Stalking Strike Force, 1997.

Wiederman, Michael W. "Sexuality Research, Institutional Review Boards, and Subject Pools." In *Protecting Human Subjects: Departmental Subject Pools and Institutional Review Boards,* edited by Garvin Chastain and R. Eric Landrum, 201–219. Washington, D.C.: American Psychological Association, 1999.

Wittmer, Denise. "Dating Violence." *Parenting of Adolescents.* <http://parentingteens.about.com/ library/weekly/aa041900a.htm? terms=dating violence> 6 December 2001.

Yllö, Kersti, and Michele Bograd, eds. *Feminist Perspectives on Wife Abuse.* Beverly Hills: Sage, 1992.

INDEX

Adolescent
Cultures,
School &
Society

Joseph L. DeVitis & Linda Irwin-DeVitis
GENERAL EDITORS

As schools struggle to redefine and restructure themselves, they need to be cognizant of the new realities of adolescents. Thus, this series of monographs and textbooks is committed to depicting the variety of adolescent cultures that exist in today's post-industrial societies. It is intended to be a primarily qualitative research, practice, and policy series devoted to contextual interpretation and analysis that encompasses a broad range of interdisciplinary critique. In addition, this series will seek to provide a pragmatic, pro-active response to the current backlash of conservatism that continues to dominate political discourse, practice, and policy. This series seeks to address issues of curriculum theory and practice; multicultural education; aggression and violence; the media and arts; school dropouts; homeless and runaway youth; alienated youth; at-risk adolescent populations; family structures and parental involvement; and race, ethnicity, class, and gender studies.

Send proposals and manuscripts to the general editors at:
Joseph L. DeVitis & Linda Irwin-DeVitis
College of Education and Human Development
University of Louisville
Louisville, KY 40292-0001

To order other books in this series, please contact our Customer Service Department at:
(800) 770-LANG (within the U.S.)
(212) 647-7706 (outside the U.S.)
(212) 647-7707 FAX

or browse online by series at:
WWW.PETERLANGUSA.COM